French Enterprise and the Challenge of the British Water Industry

Water Without Frontiers

By

MAIRI MACLEAN

Centre for Management Studies and Department of French
Royal Holloway and Bedford New College
University of London, U.K.

Avebury

Aldershot · Brookfield USA · Hong Kong · Singapore · Sydney

Published by
Avebury
Academic Publishing Group
Gower House
Croft Road
Aldershot
Hampshire GU11 3HR
England

Gower Publishing Company
Old Post Road
Brookfield
Vermont 05036
USA

A CIP catalogue record for this book is available from the British Library and the US Library of Congress.

Book design and typesetting by Philip Taylor, Royal Holloway and Bedford New College, University of London, based on a specification by Gower Publishing Company Limited. Typeset using TEX at the Computer Centre (RHBNC) in Adobe Palatino 10/12 and 9/10.8, and processed on the Linotronic 300 of the University of London Computer Centre.

ISBN 1 85628 100 0

Printed in Great Britain by
Athenaeum Press Ltd, Newcastle upon Tyne.

French Enterprise and the
Challenge of the British Water Industry

For Jolyon, Emily and Alexander

Contents

List of Figures and Tables

Acknowledgements

This book grew out of my experience as an MBA student at the University of Bath, when it began life as a summer research project. My first thanks go to Alan Butt Philip of the Centre for European Industrial Studies for the assistance and inspiration he provided as project supervisor at the time. My understanding of the water businesses of France and Britain has been sharpened by numerous interviews and conversations with French and British water chiefs and industrialists, the majority of whom prefer to remain anonymous. I would like, nevertheless, to mention Louis-Marie Pons of the Compagnie Générale des Eaux. Many others have helped, directly and indirectly, in the preparation of this volume. Special thanks are due to Sir Frederick Corfield, Q.C., Judith Eversley of the Consumers in the European Community Group, Alan Jackson of NALGO, the staff of the Department of Privatisation Services at Price Waterhouse, and also to the Institut pour une Politique Européenne de l'Environnement in Paris. The Countryside Commission, Greenpeace, the Institute for European Environmental Policy in London, the Water Companies Association and the World Wildlife Fund furnished much invaluable material and advice, for which I am grateful. The Department of French at Royal Holloway and Bedford New College, University of London, provided much needed research time. The encouragement offered by Charles Harvey and Malcolm Smith was particularly welcome. Philip Taylor of the Computer Centre made an excellent job of typesetting the manuscript.

Last but not least, Emily Kirstine and 'MBA baby' Alexander Boris deserve a special thank-you for putting up with a commuting academic for a mother. Most of all, I wish to thank my husband Jolyon, without whose help and encouragement this book would never have seen the light of day.

Glossary and Abbreviations

Abstraction	Extraction of raw water direct from source for use or treatment.
BT	British Telecom.
Catchment	Area from which a river or reservoir is fed by rainfall.
CBI	Confederation of British Industry.
CEGB	Central Electricity Generating Board (now disbanded and replaced with privately-owned companies selling electricity to monopoly regional distributors).
CGE	Compagnie Générale des Eaux.
CGT	Confédération Générale du Travail.
CLA	Country Landowners Association.
COPA II	Control of Pollution Act—Part II.
CPRE	Council for the Protection of Rural England.
DGXI	Directorate General of the European Commission. Responsible for the Environment and Nuclear Safety.
Directive	Instruction by EC to member states to legislate on a given matter within a given time span.
Discharge consent	Standards set for discharges from sewage works and industries, in order to attain proposed river quality objectives.
DoE	Department of the Environment.
EC	European Community

Ecu	European Currency Unit.
EEC	European Economic Community.
EMS	European Monetary System.
EMU	Economic and Monetary Union.
ERM	Exchange Rate Mechanism (of EMS).
Eutrophication	Multiplication of algae in water to the point at which all available oxygen is used up.
GLC	Greater London Council.
GUSTO	General Utilities Scientific and Technical Organisation, a Franco-British research club launched by Générale des Eaux.
HMIP	Her Majesty's Inspectorate of Pollution.
IMF	International Monetary Fund.
K factor	Sets the annual amount by which a water business may increase its charges in real terms — that is, above the rate of inflation — until the year 2000. K factors for water authorities were issued in July 1989, and will be reviewed in 1994; K figures for water supply companies were issued in 1990.
MAC	Maximum Admissible Concentration.
MAFF	Ministry of Agriculture, Fisheries and Food.
Mains relining	Removal of internal corrosion and introduction of mortar or other lining.
MEP	Member of European Parliament.
MMC	Monopolies and Mergers Commission.
NALGO	National Association of Local Government Officers.
NRA	National Rivers Authority.
NUPE	National Union of Public Employees.
OECD	Organisation for Economic Cooperation and Development.
Ofgas	Office of Gas Supply.
OFT	Office of Fair Trading.
Oftel	Office of Telecommunications.
Ofwat	Office of Water Services, headed by the Director General of Water Services.
PHLS	Public Health Laboratory Service.
Reasoned opinion	A view — which is not binding — expressed by the Commission on a given policy.
Regulation	A law which, once adopted by the Council of Ministers, is directly binding in all member states.

Replacement	The construction of a new sewer or water main either in the same location as the original or in a new location, incorporating the purpose of the old.
RPI	Retail price index, incorporated with K to calculate charges.
RQO	River Quality Objective.
RSPB	Royal Society for the Protection of Birds.
RWA	Regional Water Authority.
SAUR	Société d'Aménagement Urbain et Rural, subsidiary of the French construction conglomerate Bouygues.
SEA	Single European Act.
Sea outfall	Pipe through which sewage is pumped out to sea.
Sewage	Contents of sewers carrying the waterborne waste of a community.
Sewerage	System of works and channels used to carry off sewage.
Silage	Decomposing grass and other vegetable substances used as winter feed for farm animals.
Slurry	Liquid excrement of farm animals living in sheds.
SWC	Statutory Water Company.
WAA	Water Authorities Association.
WCA	Water Companies Association.
WRC	Water Research Council.
WSPLC	Water Supply plc.
WWF	World Wildlife Fund (now 'World-wide Fund for Nature').

Figure 1
The Ten Regional Water Authorities
of England and Wales, 1973–89

Figure 2
The Twenty-Eight Statutory Water Companies
in England and Wales, 1989

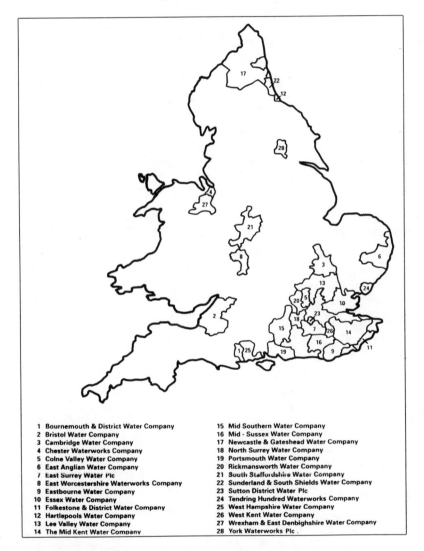

1 Bournemouth & District Water Company	15 Mid Southern Water Company
2 Bristol Water Company	16 Mid - Sussex Water Company
3 Cambridge Water Company	17 Newcastle & Gateshead Water Company
4 Chester Waterworks Company	18 North Surrey Water Company
5 Colne Valley Water Company	19 Portsmouth Water Company
6 East Anglian Water Company	20 Rickmansworth Water Company
7 East Surrey Water Plc	21 South Staffordshire Water Company
8 East Worcestershire Waterworks Company	22 Sunderland & South Shields Water Company
9 Eastbourne Water Company	23 Sutton District Water Plc
10 Essex Water Company	24 Tendring Hundred Waterworks Company
11 Folkestone & District Water Company	25 West Hampshire Water Company
12 Hartlepools Water Company	26 West Kent Water Company
13 Lee Valley Water Company	27 Wrexham & East Denbighshire Water Company
14 The Mid Kent Water Company	28 York Waterworks Plc .

Reproduced with permission from The Water Supply Companies
Factbook

1 Introduction

We never know the worth of water until the well is dry — (Kelly).

Background: the water privatisation controversy

The privatisation of the water industry in November 1989 — by which the then Conservative government under the leadership of Margaret Thatcher offered for sale to the public the utility functions of water supply, sewerage, and sewage treatment and disposal[1] carried out by the ten regional water authorities of England and Wales[2] (see Figure 1) — is the highly emotive, controversial and complex issue which forms the backcloth to this book.

The issue is an emotive one because of the widespread belief that water is somehow 'different', being God-given and essential to human life, a view which persists despite government insistence that it was not water itself which was privatised, but merely those functions necessary to bring it to homes and industries.[3]

The issue is a controversial one because of the nature of competition in the water industry. Since Mrs Thatcher's first electoral victory in 1979, the spur to efficiency which competition and consumer choice are alleged to provide has been at the heart of Conservative Party doctrine, determining in particular the government's attitude to public services. Yet water — like gas, like telecommunications — is a classic example of a natural monopoly. Unlike gas, and unlike telecommunications, however, it has no substitute. It is uniquely and overwhelmingly a monopoly.

The 1987 Conservative Election Manifesto attributed the success of previous privatisations largely to the fact that the companies concerned had been 'exposed to the full commercial discipline of the customer'.[4] There are other forms of energy, and other channels of communication from which the customer may choose. Water, however, affords no possible alternative

1

to a monopoly supply situation. The unnecessary duplication of production and distribution services would greatly increase costs if more than one supplier served a given area. Viewed in this light, the customer clearly benefits from the number of producing firms being restricted to one. But, as Pappas, Brigham and Shipley (1983) point out, where only one firm serves a market the advantage of enhanced economic efficiency may also be outweighed by economic exploitation.[5] Given that 'the consumer has no choice but to accept the service he gets and pay the price demanded',[6] monopolistic firms have the potential to earn 'excessive profits' and to underproduce.[7] 'Excessive profits' may be defined as profits so substantial that the firm earns a rate of return on capital which surpasses the risk-adjusted norm, while 'underproduction' is said to exist when production is held at a level where the cost of producing one additional unit is less than the social benefit which would derive from its production.

Were the privatised water authorities, the new water plcs, to exploit their position in the market as sole producers, they would not be alone among privatised utilities. Both British Gas and British Telecom (BT) have operated since their privatisation as private monopolies, uncurbed by a truly competitive environment. Such competition as does exist has proved too small and ineffectual to successfully bring prices down: by late 1990 British Gas still retained 98 per cent of the industrial gas market, while BT had conceded less than 5 per cent of the market to a single competitor, Mercury. It is a sad reflection on BT that telephone bills in the UK should be the highest among industrialised nations, despite the fact that the company occupies an enviable fourth place in the European league table of top profit-earning businesses.[8] A three-minute local call cost 11 pence in the UK in 1990, compared with 5.8 pence in the Federal Republic and only 5 pence in France.[9] By 1989 BT was making a profit of about £800 million a year (more than £2 million per day) on international calls. The company had also been slow to improve its service to customers. Only when Mercury produced itemised bills did BT grant that it might be possible to do so. In general, however, it has been left to the industries' watchdogs, the Office of Gas Supply (Ofgas) and the Office of Telecommunications (Oftel), to strive for the efficiency, choice and fair prices which privatisation was meant to achieve.[10]

It was as an 'antidote' to these twin threats of exploitation and underproduction that the notion of 'comparative competition' was conceived: the idea that competition in the water industry could somehow be simulated by meaningful comparisons of the performance of each of the water undertakers by the industry's regulators. As a concept, however, it was flawed from the start. If in the business of clean water supply a healthy 39 firms might be compared (the ten regional water authorities plus the 29 statutory water companies (see Figure 2),[11] the latter supplying 23 per cent of water in England and Wales to some 12 million consumers), in the treatment and disposal of dirty water there were only the ten privatised water authorities. Each, moreover, was confronted with problems so diverse in nature as to limit the value of comparing their respective performances. And if the customer might be expected to benefit from the economies of scale and consequent lower charges which would be likely to result from the merger of two or more adjoining companies, the need to keep the number of comparators artificially high was bound to militate against such cost reductions and efficiency gains.

Fears that the privatisation of water would indeed lead to sharp price rises appeared to be confirmed in January 1989, when the statutory water companies announced increases in charges of 30–50 per cent and attributed these directly to privatisation, *and this in spite of the fact that the water companies were already in private hands.*[12] But, as the term 'statutory' suggests, they had hitherto been controlled by law as to the profit they could make and the dividends they could allocate to shareholders.[13] With privatisation, however, profit control was to give way to price regulation. Cynics might therefore say that the companies were striking while the iron was hot.

Finally, the issue is a complex one because, while the sale itself is complete, the privatisation of water continues to encroach on a number of other items of 'unfinished business', each of which is controversial in its own right.

The division of the industry through the establishment of the National Rivers Authority (NRA), to be responsible for regulatory and river management functions, has emerged perhaps surprisingly as one of the least controversial of these—if only because the strengthened regulation of the industry is welcomed by industry chiefs and conservationists alike.[14]

'Trying to regulate ourselves was both impossible and intolerable', one water authority chairman told me. Acting as both gamekeeper and poacher had become increasingly untenable. The water authorities were clearly loathe to prosecute industrialists who exceeded their discharge consents —the maximum flow of sewage or trade effluent which could legally be discharged into a river or stream—when they themselves were often in breach of the law. From 1976, public expenditure cuts had hit the water industry particularly hard. Thereafter, consent standards for discharges from sewage works and industries, designed to achieve certain river quality objectives (RQOs), tended to be set according to what was considered 'achievable'. What this meant all too often in practice was that standards were constantly revised downwards, as river quality declined. In 1989 Lord Crickhowell, a former Conservative cabinet minister, was appointed Director General of the new watchdog body. Within a year, he was pressing for accelerated environmental improvements, over and above the £26 billion capital spending programme designed to put right years of infrastructural neglect. But the NRA has yet to be fully tried and tested in practice. In its commitment to water quality objectives being achieved as soon as possible, whatever the cost, the NRA is clearly at odds with the second principal regulator of the industry, the Office of Water Services (Ofwat) headed by Ian Byatt, whose primary function is to keep costs down. Which of these two watchdogs wins the day, and whether the environment is sold down the river as a result, remains to be seen. That the NRA has consistently complained of staff shortages since its foundation bodes ill for the future quality of Britain's water.

The most controversial item of 'unfinished business' is without doubt the prosecution of Britain by the European Commission for her continuing failure to fully implement through UK law the directive relating to the quality of water for human consumption (80/778/EEC).[15] The directive in question harmonises standards for assessing water quality, and sets 66 criteria or 'parameters' which cover taste and appearance as well as safety (see below, Chapter 6). Britain ought to have complied with the directive by 17 July 1985. Various derogations or exemptions had been granted, but the last of these expired in September 1989, when goodwill as well as time seemed to run out.[16] Breaches of the nitrate and lead standards reinforced the Commission's case. The prosecution of Wessex Water for concentrations of pesticides sometimes twenty-one times over the EC limit was announced in June 1991.

Action was also brought by the Commission against the UK over her implementation of the bathing water directive, more precisely over the sewage contamination of Blackpool, Southport and Formby beaches in north-west England. In general, however, this directive has been more positively received in the UK, providing a yardstick for the design and location of new sewage outfalls, and leading to research on water movements.[17] In 1987 the Water Authorities Association (WAA) introduced 'Blue Flag Awards' for Britain's cleanest beaches. Yet analogous to the misguided policy of 'tall stack' chimneys which lacked pollution controls and gave rise to acid rain, long sea outfalls which offer only primary treatment may simply send the problem further out to sea without dealing with it. It would be tragic if the price of cleaning up Britain's beaches were the further deterioration of her coastal waters. Britain intends to continue dumping sewage at sea until 1998, by which time it is estimated that a further 500 million tonnes of sludge will have been 'disposed of' in this way. And although no causal relationship between the dumping of untreated sewage at sea and the decline in our marine environment has been scientifically proven, the fact that food poisoning due to the consumption of contaminated shellfish is on the increase, doubling between 1971 and 1986 according to the Public Health Laboratory Service (PHLS), implies that one exists.[18]

The European court actions are not without justification: the outdated infrastructure and crumbling sewers which blight Britain's water industry are the result of a chronic lack of investment by successive governments. As far as sewers are concerned, 'out of sight, out of mind' has been the ruling maxim. And while it is generally recognized that the average life of a sewer is around 50 years, almost half of the sewers in England and Wales were installed prior to World War II, and as many as one-quarter pre-date World War I. The cost of compliance with European Community (EC) standards alone has been estimated by officials in the Directorate General of the European Commission responsible for the environment (DGXI) to amount to some £9 billion, a figure which government has been quick to deny.[19] Environmental economist John Bowers and his colleagues point out that within a six month period, from the winter of 1988 to the summer of 1989, the government's estimates of the costs of meeting quality standards for rivers, drinking water, beaches and bathing water escalated from a modest £2,500 million to £18,630 million (Bowers et al., 1989). Yet according to the authors, only £5,660 million of this is directly attributable to environmental costs; the remainder, they conclude, can only be accounted for by the urgent need for infrastructural renewal after more than a decade of neglect.[20] Other problems — the rising water-table of Britain's cities due to industrial decline, the recent doubling of the rat population due to warmer winters — can only add to the bill.

The controversy surrounding the privatisation of water has been further fuelled by its unfortunate timing, occurring as it did at a time when Britons and Europeans alike were finally waking up to the seriousness of global threats such as ozone depletion and greenhouse warming. Major environmental catastrophes, such as Chernobyl, the burning of the rain forest and the drying up of the Aral Sea, thrust the ecological limits to the planet into public awareness for what seemed like the first time, ending an enduring assumption that Nature would always forgive man his worst excesses. The opening up of Eastern Europe in 1989 revealed a catalogue of horrors. Forty years of the privileging of production coupled with a total disregard for the environment had given rise to levels of water and air pollution never previously encountered in the West: this was a world where the barest essentials of life — the air one breathes, the water one drinks — were dangerously contaminated. Green issues are set to dominate political agendas throughout the 1990s, when a trade-off may have to be made between economic growth on the one hand and concern for the environment on the other. It seems, then, that the privatisation of water in England and Wales threw into stark relief other major issues which transcend it in importance.

Thus it is not without good reason that this most politically sensitive of privatisations was also by far the most unpopular to date. (A successful flotation was deemed a vital prerequisite to the much bigger sale of electricity, which after seemingly endless set-backs finally took place in two stages, in the late autumn and spring of 1990–91.) Electoral hostility to the water sell-off was blamed, *inter alia*, for the mid-term downturn in the government's popularity. An opinion poll conducted by Public Attitude Surveys discovered that 58 per cent of adults (and 46 per cent of Conservative voters) believed that the privatisation of the industry would lead to a poorer service for customers. As few as 13 per cent predicted an improvement in service.[21]

The number of different issues at play in the privatisation of water contributed to a general situation of confusion, the 'muddy waters' which characterised the sale. Yet many of these issues were to some extent predictable; the EEC Directive on water quality, for instance, had been unanimously agreed by Member States in July 1980, for implementation in 1985. One issue, however, was not predictable, and in the event took almost everyone by surprise.

The French connection

There are more things in heaven and earth, Horatio, than are dreamt of in your philosophy — (Shakespeare).

In July 1977, when Britain had a Labour government under the leadership of James Callaghan, a White Paper was published which proposed the establishment of a National Water Authority with the responsibility of developing a national strategy for all water services in England and Wales. But the plan was deferred until the private water companies could be brought into public ownership, then dropped altogether when Labour lost the ensuing election.[22] British Waterways was one of several nationalised industries to lack a published financial target when the Conservatives took office in 1979.[23]

The new Conservative administration did nothing about water for four years. September 1983, however, saw a perceptible change in gear, when the government set up the Water Authorities Association and introduced businessmen (such as Nicholas Hood of Wessex, and Roy Watts of Thames), with no previous experience of water, into the industry.[24] But the new chairmen needed time to adapt themselves to a different milieu, and it would be some time before government plans for the privatisation of the industry — now in embryonic form — would see the light of day.

In 1984, when the British water industry was busy administering itself, and the British public was scarcely aware that there was a water industry to administer, the diversified French company Lyonnaise des Eaux decided to take a look at the UK water market. Established in 1880, Lyonnaise des Eaux is the second largest water supplier in France. In 1984 she was also the second largest water supplier in the world, and this in spite of the fact that water services accounted at the time for little more than 20 per cent of the group's activity.[25] By June 1988 Lyonnaise des Eaux was supplying water to some 18 million people, including eight million in the United States, Canada, Spain, Morocco and the South Pacific.[26]

What the company saw in the UK was not, however, to its taste: the leading investment bank it had commissioned to conduct the study concluded
that there was no financial interest whatsoever for a French company to
invest in the British water business.[27] The water authorities were in public
hands, and the water companies subject to such stringent financial controls that there was little incentive for efficient use of resources other than
management pride.

In February 1986, however, a White Paper was published, which outlined
government plans for the privatisation of the 10 water authorities. These
plans became firmer with the re-election of the Conservative government
in June 1987. In July, a consultation paper was published, clarifying the
government's revised proposals for the restructuring of the water authorities, under which their utility functions of supply and treatment were to be
transferred to public limited companies and offered for sale to the public.[28]
Suddenly, a whole new ball game was brought into play, rekindling the
interest of Lyonnaise des Eaux, and attracting two new French players: la
Compagnie Générale des Eaux, and la Société d'Aménagement Urbain et
Rural (SAUR), founded in 1853 and 1933 respectively.

Simon (1960) has proposed that the solution of any decision problem in
business can be viewed in four steps:

1. *Perception* of decision need or opportunity (the 'intelligence' phase).
2. *Formulation* of alternative courses of action.
3. *Evaluation* of the alternatives for their respective contribution.
4. *Choice* of one or more alternatives for implementation.[29]

What happened next suggested that, while the British had scarcely left
the starting-block (stage 1), the French were already at the finishing-post
(stage 4), underlining their strong international presence and impressive
portfolio of diversified activities with a quickness to seize 'exceptional opportunities' when these arose.[30]

June 1988 saw the first full-scale takeover of a private water company,
when Lyonnaise des Eaux successfully bid £47.6 million for Essex Water, the
largest of the statutory water companies.[31] Less than two weeks later the
group stepped up its attack on the East Anglian Water Company, in which
it already held a 28.4 per cent stake, and which it subsequently purchased
outright for £21.6 million.[32] In early October 1988 the world's largest water
distributor, France's Compagnie Générale des Eaux, joined the fray, making
agreed bids through its UK subsidiary General Utilities for Lee Valley Water
and North Surrey Water, of which at the time of purchase the group already
owned 40 and 37.1 per cent respectively.[33] The following month, SAUR,
the third largest water services group in France and, at the time, also in
the world—despite being only a subsidiary, albeit of the mighty French
construction conglomerate, Bouygues[34]—bid a grand total of £68 million

for three British water companies: Mid-Southern, Mid-Sussex and West
Kent.[35]

Other acquisitions followed, and by the spring of 1989, 12 of the 28 statutory water companies of England and Wales were owned or controlled by
French suppliers. Holdings of up to 29.9 per cent had been purchased in
a further nine.[36] *A 13 per cent share in what was after all a national resource
had been snapped up by foreign firms under the very noses of the British water
authorities,* impotent onlookers to the drama. Where public water authorities sought to protect their own interests by attempting to buy shares in the
statutory companies in their area, they were chastised by government and
prevented from retaliating. 'My only regret is that we could not respond:
there are no British players', one water authority chairman told me in a
personal interview. Some people were outraged: 'Eau no!' ran the head-
line in the *Sun*. There were accusations of a 'carve-up', which the French
groups angrily denied.[37] Others wondered why it had been allowed to happen. The British government was caught off guard, and slow to react. In
January 1989, however, an amendment to the Water Bill ruled that bids for
one or more water companies exceeding £30 million in value should be au-
tomatically referred to the Monopolies and Mergers Commission (MMC).[38]
Ownership of Britain's private water companies had become a public and
emotive issue, tinged with xenophobia.

Purpose of the study

Given the penetration of the UK market for public water supply by French
water distributors, outlined above, the primary objective of this book is to
assess the potential advantages and disadvantages for Britain of this French
presence. To this end, it addresses three key questions:

1. What is the strategic thinking behind the French interest in this sector?

2. Given that 'the firm' is not a unified entity, but rather represents in
   the terms of Cyert and March (1963) a 'coalition of different interest
   groups',[39] to what extent does the French penetration present both opportunities and threats to the various stakeholders concerned?

   — the water companies themselves
   — the newly privatised water plcs
   — the management teams of the above
   — shareholders
   — customers and taxpayers
   — unions and employees.

And if there are noticeable differences in these various perspectives,
why is this so?

3.   With the quality of life of future generations hanging in the balance, environmental issues are primordial. Few firms have chosen, as the French groups Lyonnaise des Eaux and Générale des Eaux have chosen, the 'industries of the environment'[40] as their vocation, the 'obligation of responding rapidly and massively to the imperative of safeguarding our environment' as their mission.[41] More are bound to do so in the near future, despite high entry barriers, the huge capital outlay required. Businesses which impact on the quality of our environment are, of necessity, growing businesses. Examining, then, the track record of Britain and France on both clean and dirty water, what impact is French ownership of British water likely to have on British compliance with EC directives on water quality?

In its conclusion, the book investigates the implications of this experience for the water businesses of Britain and France post-1992, and assesses their strategic opportunities and potential for expansion. Finally, it examines whether this is an isolated incident, and speculates on what the British can expect from the French in other businesses.

Scope of the study

Given the vastness and complexity of the subject of water privatisation in the UK, impinging as it does on so many other important issues, it has proved necessary to draw a tight circle around material deemed to be essential to fulfilling the specific objectives of this book, while, for reasons of clarity and economy, much of the peripheral detail has had to be left to one side. At the same time, however, the privatisation of water is an integral part of the present study. It was because of privatisation that the 'exceptional opportunities' mentioned above came into being in the first place. Privatisation will therefore be discussed in appropriate depth in Chapter 3, as part of the historical and political context. In selecting as the focus of the present study the French penetration of the British water business, however, the author, who has lived, studied and worked in France, hopes that the project will benefit from her knowledge and understanding of French society, culture and business life.

Not all limitations were self-imposed, however. Others were extraneous to the project. With only the water businesses of England and Wales being offered for sale, there were clear geographical limits to the scope of the study: separate legislation has related to the water industries of Scotland and Northern Ireland, which continue to be linked to local government.

In the run-up to privatisation, moreover, at the time when the field-work for the present book was carried out, all statements made by water authority employees of all positions on the privatisation of the industry had first to be approved by a government vetting committee, the newly established

Documentation Clearing Group, lest they 'mislead' the public. The embargo carried with it the potential penalty of a two-year prison sentence for infringement. Water authority managers were therefore understandably reluctant to accord interviews, and the author is grateful for those interviews (including one with an advisor to the government on water privatisation) she nevertheless succeeded in obtaining.

The water companies, on the contrary, were open and friendly. Some had a particular story to tell. This ease of access provided a welcome contrast to the closed doors of the water authorities. For many of the private water companies of England and Wales, the privatisation of water has meant the passing of an era stretching back in some cases to the last century. This book is also dedicated to them.

Methodology

Research carried out by the author, drawing on both primary and secondary sources (see below, Chapter 2), allowed her to reach certain preliminary conclusions to the questions outlined above. These conclusions were then revised and refined as a result of the (confidential) personal interviews she obtained with water authority chairmen, the general managers and directors of private water companies, officials at the Water Companies Association (WCA), senior executives in the French water firms, an advisor to government on water privatisation, officials at the Institut pour une Politique Européenne de l'Environnement in Paris, and other interested parties. Given the sensitivity of the subject under investigation, these interviews were by necessity unstructured. Each proved to be invaluable in its own way, yielding new insights and new ideas. But for the purposes of comparison a small core of three questions were common to all: these were the three research questions addressed by this project, and specified above. In this way, inter-firm differences in attitude to the French involvement — which public statements such as annual reports invariably seek to conceal — were highlighted.

Notes

1. For a definition of these and other terms, see Glossary and Abbreviations.

2. The 10 Water Authorities, now water services plcs, are: Anglian, Northumbrian, North West, Severn Trent, Southern, South West, Thames, Welsh, Wessex and Yorkshire. Together they are responsible for 75 per cent of the water supply and 96 per cent of sewage services in England and Wales.

3. See 'Ridley on attack as bill passes Commons stages', *Financial Times*, 5 April 1989, p. 10. The privatised functions comprise impounding, piping, pumping, treatment, maintenance and billing.

4. 1987 Conservative Election Manifesto.

5. Pappas, J. L., Brigham, E. F. and Shipley, B. (1983), *Managerial Economics*, Cassell Educational Ltd., London, p. 352.

6. Corfield, The Rt. Hon. Sir F. V. (1988), *Water Privatisation and the Consumer*, Selsdon Group, Stroud. The author — a right-wing Conservative, former member of the British Waterways Board (1974–83) and Director of Mid-Kent Water Company — voices the concern which is widespread among Conservative ranks: namely, that the newly privatised water plcs will be in a privileged position to maximise profitability at customers' expense.

7. Pappas, J. L., Brigham, E, F, and Shipley, B, op. cit., p. 352.

8. See the report on Europe's 15,000 Largest Companies (1989), published by ELC International, cited in 'Europe's top 20 businesses', *European Research*, vol. 1, part 1, January 1990.

9. Survey by efficiency consultants National Utility Services, reported in Chapman, C. (1990), *Selling the Family Silver: has privatization worked?*, Hutchinson Business Books, London.

10. For examples of the battles which Ofgas and Oftel have been forced to wage on British Gas and British Telecom respectively, see 'Ofgas presses for more competition', *Independent on Sunday*, 9 December 1990, p. 5, and 'BT forced to slash the cost of overseas calls', *Independent*, 23 December 1990, p. 1.

11. The 28 Statutory Water Companies comprise: Bournemouth and District Water, Bristol Waterworks, Cambridge Water, Chester Waterworks, Colne Valley Water, East Surrey Water, East Worcestershire Waterworks, the Eastbourne Waterworks, Essex Water, Folkestone and District, the Hartlepools Water, Lee Valley Water, the Mid-Kent Water, Mid-Southern Water, Mid-Sussex Water, Newcastle and Gateshead, North Surrey Water, Portsmouth Water, Rickmansworth Water, the South Staffordshire Waterworks, Suffolk Water (formerly the East Anglian Water Company), Sunderland and Southshields Water, Sutton District Water, Tendring Hundred Waterworks, West Hampshire Water, West Kent Water, Wrexham and East Denbighshire Water and York Waterworks Companies. Where the figure of 29 private water companies is quoted, Cholderton — which is registered as a private water company, but which serves a mere 40 houses in the Wessex area — is included in their number.

12. The Managing Director of both West Kent and Mid-Sussex Water Companies, Michael Streeter, specified in a letter to customers that as much as half of the

proposed 43 per cent rise was 'to meet privatisation requirements'. (See 'Water company blames price rise on privatisation', *Financial Times*, 1 March 1989, p. 12.). The private water companies later agreed to reduce their proposed increases to an average of 22 per cent.

13. The stringent financial constraints governing the private water companies, as contained in the Waterworks Code of the 1945 Water Act, are: statutory control on the maximum rate of dividend; share capital must be issued by tender; limits on reserve and contingency funds; and limits on the carrying forward of surpluses to succeeding years. See the report by UBS Phillips and Drew (1989), *The Water Industry in England and Wales*, p. 46.

14. The Countryside Commission welcomes the advent of the new regulatory authority in its publication *Water: the case for the countryside* (1988), Countryside Commission, Cheltenham.

15. EC, *Official Journal* reference L229 30.8.80. For a useful and comprehensive discussion of the directive and its effect on UK practice see Haigh, N. (1987), *EEC Environmental Policy and Britain*, 2nd ed., Longman, Harlow, pp. 42–50, and Consumers in the European Community Group (1987), *The Quality of Drinking Water: a consumer view*, CECG, London, pp. 2–11.

16. For a summary of the principal infringements, see 'Patten acts to placate EC over water quality', *Financial Times*, 19 September 1989, p. 10.

17. See Haigh, N., op. cit., p. 67.

18. For a detailed discussion of the effects of sewage dumping at sea on our marine environment, see Rose, C. (1990), *The Dirty Man of Europe: the great British pollution scandal*, Simon and Schuster, London.

19. 'EC standards "may cost water industry £9bn."', *Financial Times*, 31 March 1989, p. 1.

20. See Bowers, J. et al. (1989), *Liquid Costs: an assessment of the environmental costs of the water industry*, WWF and Media Natura, Leeds, p. 8.

21. See 'Consumers still fear privatisation', *Guardian*, 17 May 1989. Research conducted by the Consumers Association further illustrated the deep-seated suspicion to the sale. A customer survey carried out by one water company confirmed this.

22. Fraser, R., ed. (1988). *Privatization: the UK Experience*, Longman, Harlow, p. 93.

23. Pappas, J. L., Brigham, E. F. and Shipley, B., op. cit., p. 505.

24. Personal interview with the General Manager of a statutory water company.

25. By 1989 water represented over 50 per cent of the group's activity: an increase of 30 per cent for which Lyonnaise des Eaux's British acquisitions were largely responsible.

26. Annual Report of the Groupe Lyonnaise des Eaux for the year 1988.

27. See 'Why a French supplier is bubbling with enthusiasm for British water', *Financial Times*, 7 April 1989, p. 17.

28. On the stage-by-stage formulation of government plans to privatise the water industry, see Fraser, R., op. cit., pp. 92–3.

29. Simon, H. A. (1960), *The New Science of Management Decision*, Harper and Row, New York, cited in Ansoff, I. (1965), *Corporate Strategy*, Penguin Books, Harmondsworth, pp. 38–9.

30. This was how Générale des Eaux described the privatisation of the British water industry in its 1988 Annual Report.

31. See 'French bid £48m for Essex Water', *Guardian*, 22 June 1988, p. 9.

32. 'French giants eye up UK water industry', *Independent*, 8 October 1988, p. 21.

33. 'Two water firms fall to the French', *Independent*, 8 October 1988.

34. SAUR was acquired by Bouygues in 1984, as part of the company's diversification strategy. See Barbanel, A. and Menanteau, J. (1987), *Bouygues: l'Empire moderne*, Ramsay, Paris, p. 221.

35. See 'French bids value water companies at £68m', *Financial Times*, 24 November 1988, p. 34.

36. Report by UBS Phillips and Drew, op. cit, pp. 46–7.

37. See 'French deny water "carve-up"', *Financial Times*, 25 January 1989, p. 20.

38. 'Ruling issued on water competition', *Financial Times*, 17 January 1989, p. 22.

39. Cyert, R. M. and March, J. G. (1963), *Behavioural Theory of the Firm*, Prentice Hall International, Hemel Hempstead.

40. Lyonnaise des Eaux Annual Report 1989, p. 2.

41. ibid., p. 4.

2 France, Britain and Water: work in progress

Every country has the history of its geography — (Vidal de la Blache).

The purpose of this chapter is to provide an overview of related and relevant research, and to indicate in what way the present study may make a contribution. This literature review neither aims nor claims to be exhaustive; it seeks instead to provide a coherent synthesis of the insights and conclusions contained in those sources — both primary and secondary — which have been found to be useful.

The business context to the topic under discussion comprises three fundamental elements, each with its own body of research. The literature review which follows proposes to discuss these three frameworks sequentially before turning to the primary focus of this report: the French penetration of the British water industry. It is appropriate to speak here of 'contexts' or of 'frameworks' because comparatively little (with the exception of newspaper articles) has been found to be of direct relevance, whereas much is indirectly related. The author has therefore attempted to sift through some of the literature which is on the boundary of her immediate subject, in search of information and insights which may help to shed light on the topic under discussion.

First, this is an 'episode' which is playing itself out in the context of the much more historically important 'drama' of the completion of the single European market. The internal market is a huge and multi-dimensional subject — embracing economic, monetary, political, even defence and security affairs — which is currently spawning a vast amount of literature, not least because its final contours have yet to emerge (Maclean and Howorth, 1991). Two of its multifarious aspects are of particular concern here. The first is the increasing number of European-wide mergers and acquisitions taking place as the final count-down to 1992 commences (Woolcock, 1989)[1], and the need for these to be effectively policed by the Community on the grounds that where major companies of more than one member state are concerned, national legislation alone is inadequate. At the time of the French penetration of the water industry, a coherent EC-wide anti-trust system was not yet in place, despite French attempts to install one before the termination of their presidency of the Commission at the end of December 1989.[2] But they *did* succeed — just as their term of office expired — in securing the agreement of the Council of Ministers to a proposal for the control of substantial mergers and acquisitions within the Community. The EC's first merger control regulation, which finally came into force in September 1990 after seventeen years of negotiation and compromise, is discussed below. On the environmental plane, of concern are also the difficulties involved in implementing that legislation which has already been agreed (Butt Philip, 1988; Haigh, 1987; Siedentopf and Ziller, 1988).[3] The effect of EC environmental policy on practice in Britain and France, and in particular the impact of those directives which relate to water quality, comes under scrutiny (CECG, 1987; Haigh, 1987; HMSO, 1989; WAA, MAFF, 1989).[4]

Our second context is that of the cultural specificities of business and economics with regard to Britain and France (Barsoux and Lawrence, 1990; Hall, 1986; Hayward, 1976, 1986; Lane, 1989).[5] These nations have very different attitudes to management and to Europe, and in order that the reader may have more of a cultural 'feel' for the economic actors concerned, a brief discussion of those 'differences which make a difference' (Bateson, 1972) is proposed.[6]

Europe is first and foremost a plurality, and is likely to remain so (Sharp and Shearman, 1987).[7] It is, as one French senior manager expressed it in a personal interview, 'a mosaic of little stones with a bit of cement around them rather than the monolithic bloc it ought to be'.[8] It was precisely as a Europe of nation states, *l'Europe des patries*, that de Gaulle first conceived of a united Europe.[9] Cries for the protection of the nation state are almost bound to continue to ring forth (especially from British soil) for some years to come. That national sovereignty should not be eroded by the creeping bureaucracy of an ever more centralised European Commission was the message of Margaret Thatcher's notorious Bruges speech, delivered in September 1988. In the end, of course, it was Mrs Thatcher's uncompromising stance over Europe which led to her undoing. Future generations, however, are likely to judge the success of the Community *by its ability to work with and manage its own diversity* — an essential prerequisite to the ultimate fulfilment of the Treaty of Rome, signed in March 1957, which 'determined to lay the foundations of an ever-closer union among the peoples of Europe'.[10] But to be taken on board, difference must first be understood.

Privatisation provides our third context. Privatisation was an international trend of the eighties which continued into the nineties, when even the countries of the Eastern bloc drew up and began to implement large-scale plans for the privatisation of public assets and industries. Austria, Belgium, Germany, Greece, Italy, the Netherlands, Norway, Portugal, Spain, Turkey and the USSR have all seen a marked contraction of their public sector. But nowhere was this trend more pronounced than in Britain and France under the respective governments of Margaret Thatcher (1979-90) (Chapman, 1990)[11] and Jacques Chirac (1986-88) (Bizaguet, 1988; de Belot, 1987; Maclean, 1987, 1989).[12] The French firms of which we speak here benefitted from the sale of public sector companies both in Britain and in France. They bought sizeable stakes in British Gas in 1986, and in their own backyard were invited to play a prominent role in the notorious *noyaux durs* or 'hard cores' of investors, created by former Finance Minister Edouard Balladur to provide newly privatised firms with an anchor for the period of transition following their change of status. So, at the time of the privatisation of the water industry in England and Wales in 1989, our French actors were already alive to the opportunities which privatisation could bring. Water privatisation has potential consequences for the consumer (Corfield, 1988), for the investor (UBS Phillips and Drew, 1989) and for the environment (Bowers et al., 1988; Countryside Commission, 1988),[13] and these will be discussed in turn.

Lastly, we shall turn to the water industries of Britain and France, highlighting their fundamental differences, and to the firms themselves, scrutinising their annual reports and public statements for evidence of those differences of capability and culture which might make a difference in the years following privatisation and the completion of the single market. This final category of literature includes mainly primary sources: annual reports, company newsletters, letters to shareholders, water share literature, advertisements and so on. While some work has been done on the preparation of the water industry for privatisation (Rees and Synnott, 1986)[14] and on water privatisation itself (Chapman, 1990), as yet no major study has been conducted into the issue which concerns us here—the French interest in British water, sparked off as a result of government plans to privatise the industry—with the exception of two reports on the French water industry by NALGO and NUPE.

In the autumn of 1988 the UK water industry trade unions dispatched delegations to Paris to meet representatives of both the French water companies and the communist-dominated labour confederation, the Confédération Générale du Travail (CGT), in order to ascertain the nature and intentions of the predators. The reports they produced on their return shed as much light on their own attitude to the buyers as on the buyers themselves. In addition, numerous newspaper and magazine articles appearing in the *Daily Telegraph*, the *Financial Times*, the *Guardian*, the *Independent*, the *Observer*, *The Economist* and even in the tabloid press—have discussed and often dramatized the issue. So too has the French press, *Le Monde* and *L'Expansion* in particular. But rarely has their coverage been of more than one page. It is this gap which the present book aims to fill.

Community merger regulation and the French

EC regulation of large mergers and acquisitions, which came fully into force on 21 September 1990 after almost two decades of intra-Community wrangling, had long been a matter of some urgency. It was increasingly seen as a prerequisite to the completion of the single market, the cornerstone of which is competition. It had become necessary to control — if not to stem — the tide of takeovers sweeping Europe as capital flows were liberalised and investment abroad became an easy means of securing market share. By 1990 around 350 European firms were changing hands every three months, at a total value of around $27 billion per quarter.[15] In a complex, uncertain world, where technological supremacy with its enormous capital cost is the key to keeping ahead of one's opponents, size matters more than ever.

Interestingly, size matters particularly to the French. An aspiration to attain *une taille critique*, a critical size for survival, prosperity and above all safety from hostile takeovers, characterised France's big companies in the run-up to 1992. A 1989 survey of 300 large and medium-sized French industrial and service firms commissioned by the Ministry of Industry revealed size to be the number one strategic objective for 38 per cent of the sample, ahead of return on capital.[16] The implication is that French companies might be willing to sacrifice some measure of profitability for the sake of growth. The companies concerned expected most of their growth (75 per cent) to be external, through acquisitions, and 70 per cent of those to concern a foreign prey. In 1989, a staggering 1,721 successful takeover bids were launched by French firms, 480 on foreign soil, and 73 per cent of this number in Europe. France had emerged, perhaps surprisingly, as the major cross-border acquirer in the Community. The 1980s ended in a wave of acquisitions. Almost half of France's top 70 companies (43 per cent) launched a successful takeover bid during the last two bumper years of the decade.[17] The new legislation gave the Commission authority over all mergers within the Community where the global turnover of the companies concerned surpasses Ecu 5 billion (approximately £3.45 billion), or where their combined turnover within the EC exceeds Ecu 250 million. This is therefore a 'one-stop' control system: national governments have no jurisdiction whatsoever over those mergers which fall under the Commission's remit. Smaller acquisitions, however, are left to the control of national bodies, such as Britain's Office of Fair Trading (OFT) and Monopolies and Mergers Commission. An 85-man task-force set up by the Commission's Competition Directorate (DGIV) has one month in which to scrutinise the markets affected by a merger, and then a further four months to reach a decision should it decide to pursue its enquiry. The acid test which determines whether or not a merger may proceed is its effect on competition, defined by Competition Commissioner Sir Leon Brittan as 'the guiding force of economic life'.[18] Article 86 of the Treaty of Rome prohibits firms from abusing a position of dominance in the market. The Commission must therefore decide whether the merger in question creates or strengthens a dominant market position to the detriment of effective competition either within the common market as a whole or within a substantial part of it. The point at which concentration becomes unacceptable occurs when more than 25 per cent of market share is involved.

However, the new merger policy had no sooner been agreed than a number of charges were levied at it. Charges which concerned the height at which the threshold had been set: as few as 50 mergers per year have the necessary combined turnover to qualify for EC vetting (although the limit is expected to be lowered to Ecu 2 billion by the end of 1993). It goes without saying that the deals with which we are concerned here would certainly have failed to be considered by Brussels despite the 'splash' they made in Britain. Moreover, what jurisdiction the Commission might have over mergers between large American or Japanese groups with substantial business interests in the Community remains a matter of ambiguity and a source of tension. The purchase by Fujitsu of an 80 per cent stake in ICL in August 1991 — one month before the new system came into effect — clearly had considerable impact in the UK, where ICL was the only major computer manufacturer. Yet in spite of the fact that ICL was also the EC's most successful producer, the deal would have been unlikely to come under scrutiny, first for reasons of size and market share, and second because of its international scope.[19] There is no doubt, however, that Europe's computer manufacturers are much the poorer for the deal having been allowed to proceed.

The Single European Act and the environment

The official documentation of the European Commission reflects the supranational approach assumed by its originating body, and retains something of the utopian tone of the Treaty of Rome. Its emphasis is on the future benefits of a harmonious union, gains which are contrasted with the monumental costs of the fragmented market of 'Non-Europe', first outlined in Albert and Ball's report in 1983[20] (Cecchini, 1988; periodicals from the European Documentation Series, 1987–90).[21]

But this almost Rousseauist discourse, which aims to transcend the factional interests of individual nation states by seeking to interpret the 'general will' of Europe, does not always find an echo in the non-verbal language of practical implementation (Butt Philip, 1988; Haigh, 1987; Sieden-topf and Ziller, 1988). And action, it is said, speaks louder than words.

In the 1980s water quality came to the fore as a central environmental issue, and sales of bottled water soared as a result. In 1977, 6 million bottles of water were drunk in the UK at a total cost of £3.5 million. By 1985, 80 million bottles were drunk, worth £48 million.[22] From 1986–88 the market increased by 145 per cent,[23] and by 1989 Britons were spending as much as £135 million per year on bottled water.[24] Recently published Community-wide research on the working of European policies at grass roots level (Butt Philip, 1987; Siedentopf and Ziller, 1988) does not accord much emphasis to those EC measures which concern the protection of the natural environment, perhaps because they are relatively new.[25] Additional research into the implementation of the EC directives on water quality[26] has come from government departments and other interested parties with a particular *parti pris* in the subject: the Consumers in the European Community Group (CECG), the Council for the Protection of Rural England (CPRE), the Institute for European Environmental Policy (IEEP), the Ministry of Agriculture, Fisheries and Food (MAFF), the Royal Society for the Protection of Birds (RSPB), the Water Authorities Association (WAA), the World Wildlife Fund (WWF). There is at present no EC inspectorate to monitor how directives are implemented in the various member states. Implementation is defined by the Commission extremely narrowly, as the translation of the directive in question into national law rather than its practical application. While it is customary for letters of compliance to be sent by individual member states to notify the Commission of the practical steps they have taken, such notification is not always obligatory, and lapses in practical compliance are investigated by the Commission only when these are drawn to its attention (Haigh, 1987).[27] According to the *Financial Times*, France, Belgium and Italy as well as Britain are being taken to the European Court of Justice over their alleged violation of the drinking water directive. Germany and Denmark have received 'reasoned opinions', where the Commission expresses a view which is not, however, binding. Meanwhile France, Belgium, Denmark, Germany, the Netherlands, Ireland, Spain and the UK have received letters from the Commission concerning alleged bathing water violations. In this, Britain may be to some extent the victim of her own honesty (as the water authorities have claimed), or of her own contrariness: officials in the Directorate General of the European Commission responsible for the environment (DGXI) report that complaints about drinking water come almost solely from the British — about their own water, and when they venture abroad, about that of other EEC countries! (CECG, 1987).[28]

Research on the implementation of EC directives on the environment, and on water quality in particular, is perhaps bound to remain fragmentary, incomplete or coloured by special pleading of various sorts while feedback provided by a supranational authority for inspection is lacking. The simultaneous lack of any *feedforward* control has no doubt introduced bias into the interpretation of directives by member states in the first place. That the bathing water directive (76/160/EEC) left members free to designate their own bathing beaches resulted in the UK declaring fewer than land-locked Luxembourg: a mere 27 for the whole of the British Isles (Bowers et al., 1988; Haigh, 1987).[29] In all of Scotland and Northern Ireland, not one single bathing beach had been identified. The threat of infringement proce-dures by the Commission, however, persuaded the British government to find another 362.

One of the arguments used extensively by critics of the EC directives on water quality is that conditions vary so much between member states that it is impossible for uniform standards to be set (CECG, 1987). After all, each country is to some extent the product of its own geography. Thus, Britain, with her short, fast rivers, sluiced out by a turbulent, tidal sea, might be said to have an obvious self-interest in not accepting emission standards for water set with reference to, say, the Rhine, which serves and drains many industrial areas in Germany and the Netherlands. Nigel Haigh (1987) underlines the significance of this point:

> Britain for pollution purposes, it can be argued, is well favoured by geog-raphy just as for transport purposes or, more facetiously, for the purposes of growing lemons, it is disadvantaged by geography. Since Italian lemon growers take advantage of the sun that geography brings them, and grow lemons rather than engage in some other activity for that very reason, and since German industrialists benefit from proximity to continental markets as a result of geography, so also it is argued that Britain should quite prop-erly profit from the ability to locate industries on estuaries or on the coast where acute pollution problems are less likely to arise and where the sea water can assimilate or destroy the pollutants.[30]

But the European Commission has set uniform standards for all. More importantly, Britain has *agreed* to these standards. Greater involvement in negotiations at the outset might have spared Britain complicated manoeu-vring when deadlines expired. At the time of writing, an EC attack on Britain's installation of long sea outfalls, spear-headed by Belgium, France, the Netherlands and Germany, each of which has a shallow sea shelf, is likely.[31] The new sea outfalls—forty-four of them, at an estimated overall cost of £100 million—are being installed so that Britain might comply with the EC bathing water directive by 1995. Yet a new EC directive 'concerning the protection of fresh, coastal and marine waters against pollution caused by nitrates from diffuse sources'—precisely those waters which sea outfalls will further pollute—has already been drafted.[32] One is reminded of the 'old woman who swallowed a fly'.

Cultural specificities: differing attitudes to Europe and to business in Britain and France

Differing attitudes to Europe

This partisan stance assumed by the British — detectable also in the them-and-us, eat-or-be-eaten tone which occasionally characterises the documentation on 1992 published by the Department of Trade and Industry (DTI)[33] — is perhaps not entirely surprising. As Alan Butt Philip suggests, 'Born-again integrationists [...] would do well to ponder how and why the plans for an internal market, and much else, in the EEC Treaty of 1957 failed to be realized by the time of the 1980s'.[34]

The French geographer Vidal de la Blache once said that 'each country has the history of its geography'. The different approaches to Europe adopted by Britain and France would seem to bear witness to the truth of this observation.

A late comer to the Community, well known as a reluctant and difficult member, Britain has clung to an old island mentality of 'splendid isolation', while slipping further down the path towards economic decline. By the late 1980s, however, British attitudes to Europe had begun to change — not sweepingly but nevertheless significantly — in favour of greater cooperation with Europe. A Gallup poll conducted at the time of the June 1989 European elections discovered that a majority of Britons (55 per cent) considered EC membership to be a 'good thing' (the highest score recorded since Britain's entry into the Community in 1973), while 72 per cent of interviewees saw no alternative to full participation in the EC if Britain's prosperity and position in the world were to be safeguarded.[35] Conservative campaign leaders, however, badly misjudged the prevailing mood in the country in 1989. The unfortunate advertisement, 'Stay at home on June 15th, and you will live on a diet of Brussels', badly backfired when Tory voters did precisely that. The Conservative vote collapsed, leaving the 32 Conservative Members of the European Parliament (MEPs) who remained feeling betrayed by their own party. A rift had clearly opened up among Conservative ranks between those who supported Mrs Thatcher's view of a Europe of sovereign states as outlined in her 1988 Bruges speech, and those who did not.[36] Ranged against her were former prime minister Ted Heath and a growing number of ex-Cabinet ministers, including her erstwhile Defence Secretary Michael Heseltine, the lion who was soon to make the kill for another to enjoy.

Britain's entry into the exchange rate mechanism (ERM) of the European Monetary System (EMS) at the beginning of October 1990 was generally seen as 'too little too late' both by the business community it was intended to placate, and by growing sections of the electorate who wanted to play a greater role in the construction of Europe *when it mattered*, rather than after the event, when the rules of the game had already been agreed. But the level at which sterling joined the ERM, suggested that entry had been little more than a cosmetic change, designed to woo voters rather than to mark a change of heart. The pound was to be kept strong, and exports expensive. That there had indeed been no change of heart — at least on Mrs Thatcher's part — was confirmed only days later when, at the Rome Summit, the then prime minister, with 'finger wagging and [...] passionate no, no, no',[37] ridiculed the idea of a single currency, dismissed the notion of an independent European central bank, rejected any move toward closer European cooperation. At Rome, Mrs Thatcher painted herself into a corner. Out of touch with public sentiment over Europe after more than eleven years as prime minister, possessed of what Sir Geoffrey Howe later described as a 'nightmare image' of a continent 'positively teeming with ill-intentioned people scheming, in her words, "to extinguish democracy", "to dissolve our national identities", to lead us "through the back door into a federal Europe"', Mrs Thatcher's lonely stand in Rome became an even lonelier one back home.

What will be the future role for Britain in Europe, as 1992 beckons? Immediately upon securing his succession to Downing Street, John Major strove to portray himself as his own man, not just the faithful chauffeur to a formidable 'backseat driver', but rather as someone who firmly believed that Britain could not influence the building of Europe from the terraces; she had to be out there on the pitch, playing hard. It remains to be seen, however, whether this change of tone will be coupled with a change of substance. The tricky task of steering through the single currency negotiations a Conservative party increasingly intent on demonstrating its own disarray was not an easy one to assume in the last eighteen months of office. The attitude towards Europe, both of the British political class and of the general public, remains fundamentally ambivalent. They fully recognise the importance of the stakes, but cannot somehow quite bring themselves to enter into the spirit of Euro-construction. An survey of European attitudes to the proposed single currency carried out in June 1991 and published in the *European* found only 37 per cent in favour in the UK (and 51 per cent against) compared with an average of 68 per cent in favour elsewhere in the Community. As has so often been the case in the past, at the end of the day, pragmatism is likely to triumph over lack of historical imagination. But at what price for Britain's future place in the new Europe?

One reason why France is such a *committed* Community member in marked contrast to Britain is precisely because she has seen Europe as a means to achieving *national* objectives. Geographically, it could be said, she has nowhere else to go — except, perhaps, North Africa, and markets have contracted there in recent years (Holcblat and Tavernier, 1989).[38] Her former colonies to the south are now seen as more of a latent threat than as cultural outposts or market outlets: Muslim fundamentalism is sweeping the Maghreb, whose populations are growing strongly.

It has not been easy for France to accept the diminished role of a second class power which the post-war world has offered her. But she has been quick to realise that French and European interests share much common ground, and that through playing a leading and constructive part in the Community, she can transcend her national limitations and enjoy an amplified role on the world stage, thus retaining more control over her own destiny than geopolitical and historical considerations alone would logically have allowed. So while many of the goals sought by France's leaders since the Liberation — welfare, security and even independence — can clearly no longer be reached through national action alone, France has nevertheless recognised that these might still be reachable at the level of Europe (Hoffmann, 1987).[39] François Mitterrand made this explicit in a much-quoted address to the French nation on 31 December 1986, when he said: 'France is our country, Europe is our future'.[40] Even Jacques Delors, who, as President of the European Commission might be assumed to be above expressions of nationalist sentiment, has published a book entitled precisely *La France par l'Europe* (1988), 'France *through* Europe'.[41] So Britain is not alone in striking a nationalist pose. But how much more constructive is that adopted by our nearest neighbour: 'in the driving seat' together with Germany rather than 'at the back of the train', as we are.[42]

Differing attitudes to business and economics

The argument which Peter Hall advances in his major work *Governing the Economy: the politics of state intervention in Britain and France* (1986) is essentially twofold. On the one hand, Hall demonstrates the cultural specificities of economics, showing how the distinct cultural patterns which permeate the socio-political fabrics of Britain and France reassert and renew themselves constantly, like old myths that never die. Thus far, he agrees with Jack Hayward (1976), who seeks to explain the success of French planning relative to British attempts in terms of 'the operation of culturally-based dominant values that inhibit or preclude some kinds of government action and favour others'.[43]

But Hall goes further, stressing at the same time that the economic legacies of our respective pasts are *not* cast in tablets of stone: 'Economic performance is not entirely a matter of fate or the product of iron laws in economics. The institutions that affect the performance of the economy are ultimately artifacts of political action. They were constructed out of political struggles, and from time to time, we may recast them'.[44] Lane (1989) supports Hall on this (but not on everything), summing up her discussion of business organisations in France, Britain and Germany with the observation: 'It cannot be denied, to paraphrase Marx, that circumstances transmitted from the past constitute powerful limitations on present endeavours to change society but equally, it must be borne in mind that people make their own history'.[45]

From the late 1970s and throughout the 1980s, France seemed indeed to go some way towards refashioning the political institutions which determine her economic performance. As Bayliss and Butt Philip (1980) point out, by the late 1970s even the French civil service, renowned for its red tape, was beginning to lose faith in *dirigisme*, and to move in a more liberal direction. During the course of the 1980s, attitudinal upheavals have transformed French business culture. A seemingly innate aversion to the risks associated with liberal private enterprise on the part of French people, fuelled by a strong Marxist tradition, appears to have gradually given way to an increasing receptivity to the culture of business enterprise (Frommer and McCormick, 1989).[46] The results of a 1983 *Figaro*-SOFRES opinion poll suggested that whereas the terms 'socialism', 'nationalisation', 'trade unionism' and 'planning' had all declined in popularity, those of 'competition', 'liberalism' and especially 'profit' were in the ascendant (Berger, 1987).[47] In a best-seller appropriately entitled *Le Métier de patron* ('How to be a boss'), Jean-Louis Servan-Schreiber, editor of France's most successful business magazine, *L'Expansion*, was able to write in 1990, 'C'est bien d'être patron. Enfin!': 'At long last it's good to be a boss!'[48]

Mitterrand himself had endorsed this new shift in values as early as January 1984, when he pronounced that, henceforth, France's position in the world hierarchy would depend first and foremost on the efforts and well-being of her business entreprise (Machin and Wright, 1985)[49] rather than on the state, the traditional support system for both winners and losers. Yet in ceding its place on centre stage to the institution of free enterprise, the state has not let go entirely. It remains in the wings, ready to intervene if necessary to correct the short-sightedness and short-termism of individual firms and markets, thus ensuring a continuing long-term perspective and an enduring responsibility.[50]

This new business orientation, together with an acceptance of state intervention when needed, is a powerful combination. Thatcher's Britain had little of the latter, and apparently not enough of the former to compensate, as was made explicit in November 1989 when the former prime minister announced a year's delay in the completion of the Channel Tunnel (a British Rail-SNCF collaborative project) due to lack of funds and rising costs. But the tunnel, at least, was eventually completed. At the time of writing, Britain's high-speed Channel tunnel rail link lies foundering on the beaches of Kent for want of government foresight and subsidy, albeit amid rumours of an eleventh-hour reprieve. As to whether John Major's attitude to public services differs significantly from that of his predecessor, we shall just have to 'wait and see'. The notion that it is not up to government to supply money for investment in public utilities was so deeply-rooted in the political culture — defined by Verba (1965) as 'the subjective orientation to politics'[51] — of the then Conservative government as to make the privatisation of the water industry, which had endured many years of capital neglect, virtually a foregone conclusion.[52]

Privatisation *Italich.*

One of the key objectives of the present study is to consider who, of the various stakeholders concerned, will be losers and who the beneficiaries of the French interest in British water. Here, we examine the conclusions drawn by academics, government departments and other interested parties as to who are likely to gain and who to lose from the privatisation of water itself, with particular reference to: the consumer, the investor and the environment.

Sir Frederick Corfield's analysis (1988) of the government's proposals for water privatisation — as laid out in the White Paper 'Privatisation of the Water Authorities in England and Wales' (Cmnd. 9734) published in February 1986 — embraces the cause of the consumer. That he opens his discussion by acknowledging his whole-hearted support for privatisation in general makes his *lack* of support for this particular privatisation all the more noteworthy. Sir Frederick's argument concerns the nature of competition in the industry (see above, Chapter 1): that the supply of water, which is essential to life and without substitute, is overwhelmingly a monopoly, and that it is therefore inappropriate to subject it to market discipline.

For market rigour will naturally demand that the water plcs earn a return on capital comparable to that available elsewhere. And as Rees and Synnott (1986) underline, this is fundamentally incompatible with objectives such as strict price controls and the need to ensure that the country's long-term infrastructure needs are met.[53] That the outlook for the consumer, in terms of what he will have to pay for his service, is bleak indeed is confirmed by UBS Phillips and Drew, who see little remaining potential for cost effective operating gains following the large real reductions of the 1980s, achieved while the industry was still under public ownership. In a letter addressed to the *Guardian*, an eminent American scholar, Daniel A. Okun, outlined the problem posed by the White Paper as one of trying to fix something which was not even broken: 'If it ain't broke, don't fix it'. Okun, who had studied the regionalisation programme since its inception in 1973, concludes: 'A sound organization for providing water-related services to the people of England and Wales now exists and it is constantly being made more efficient with improved levels of service. Why tamper with it?'[54]

The consumer's loss may prove to be the shareholder's gain. UBS Phillips and Drew announce 'substantial upside possibilities' for the investor. As for the downside, they conclude 'there is none'.[55] But this gain depends directly on any extra costs which may be arise — and which were not included in the original 'K' negotiations[56] — being passed on to the customer. 'Cost pass-through' as it is termed clearly gives the new water plcs an in-built advantage. It is a guarantee against adversity, something other firms in financial and equity markets do not possess. Examining which particular items of expenditure by water plcs are eligible for 'cost pass-through' as it is termed, Bowers et al. (1989) find the list to be 'all embracing' — cold comfort for customers indeed.[57]

The environment might also benefit from privatisation. UBS Phillips and Drew claim that 'Had the industry remained in the public sector, there is no doubt [. . .] that compliance [with EC directives] would have been a great deal longer in coming — essentially due to political reluctance to increase prices too quickly'.[58] Unfortunately, neither the CPRE, nor the RSPB, nor the WWF, nor even the Countryside Commission (the government's official adviser on countryside issues) share this confidence. The Countryside Commission (1988) criticises the Water Bill for the imprecision of several of its clauses. Under Clause 7(4), for example, the NRA is obliged to promote conservation only 'to the extent that it considers desirable'. Bowers et al. (1987, 1988a, 1988b)[59] draw attention to the significant environmental problems which are likely to arise from the utilisation or sale of redundant assets such as reservoirs and land holdings. Wildlife habitats, they claim, are almost bound to suffer, particularly since according to UBS Phillips and Drew non-core activities will be worthwhile *only where these are substantial.*

Cultural specificities of the water industries in Britain and France

First we shape our structures, and afterwards they shape us
— (Winston Churchill).

Examination of the French water industry, as it is presented in both *Le Livre bleu de l'eau potable* (1980), published by the French water undertakers union, the Syndicat Professionnel des Distributeurs d'Eau, and NALGO's report on the French 'invaders' (1988), throws into sharp relief the following salient features:

— The French water companies have no asset base in France: they are *sociétés distributrices*, licensed to use for the purposes of distribution assets which belong to others — specifically to the French municipalities.

— This affects the nature of competition in the industry. Since the private companies do not generally own the infrastructure, but merely earn the right to use it, real competition *does* exist between contenders for contracts without any duplication of networks.

— Water has never been nationalised in France; and this in spite of the fact that France has the greatest public sector outside the Eastern bloc.

— The French take a long-term view. Contracts may be agreed for up to thirty years. Contracts are of four key types:

concession (30 years), where the municipality cedes entire responsibility for water supply to the contractor;

franchise (15 years), a service operation contract of around where the contractor operates and maintains plants owned by the municipality;

gérance (12 years), a billing arrangement, where the contractor collects charges on a cost plus fee basis;

service (5 years), where the contractor furnishes a specific service, such as meter-reading, again on a cost plus fee basis.

— Additionally, there is a recognition in France that good quality water *costs*.

— There is a recognition that *one should pay for what one consumes*; so metering is commonplace, and transport costs and even a cleaning-up charge are included in the price.

— The French operate a decentralised system with a strong local base.

— It is taken for granted that the companies should use this local base to promote their other activities.

— So commonplace is diversification that water supply and sewerage services normally account for less than 50 per cent of a French water distributor's activity, and sometimes as little as 20 per cent.

This contrasts markedly with a British water industry:

— Which *does* own its assets, including 500,000 acres of land.

— Where the consumer has no choice but to accept the local supplier (still the case irrespective of privatisation).

— Where the emphasis has been on the short term, retarding much-needed infrastructural investment.

— Where price does not reflect consumption (first because water is still largely unmetered, and second because charges are based on the rateable value of houses, and will continue to be so until the end of the century).

— Where it is understood that water, being free, should be available to all at very little cost (prior to privatisation, Britain had the lowest water charges of Europe).

— Where water authorities and companies have tended to assume a low profile.

— Where diversification, prior to privatisation, was virtually non-existent.

The net result of these fundamental differences seems to be two singularly different philosophies. The annual reports of Générale des Eaux and Lyonnaise des Eaux tell of acquisition strategies pursued, of springboards for European and global expansion, of being firmly positioned in long-term growth markets. And while the business of business may well be business, it is only in the last few years that their British counterparts — invisible actors prevented by law from engaging in other activities *even if they had so wished* — have begun to see themselves as 'businesses' at all.

Traditionally, strategy has been viewed as the response of an organisation to its environment. Thus, writers have tended to focus on government legislation or economic forces, external to the firm, as impeding or facilitating change. Within the firm, the emphasis was on organisational resources, such as finance or managerial competence.

But this is only part of the story, which ignores a major influence on strategy formulation which has to do with the strategy makers themselves. As Johnson and Scholes point out, it is too simple to think of strategy as purely a response to the environment; for it is clear that, confronted with similar environments, organisations will respond differently (Johnson and Scholes, 1988).[60] More recently, writers and researchers have sought to understand why some businesses have performed consistently better than others, and some have reached the conclusion that 'processes of strategic management need to be understood as an essentially cultural process' (Clutterbuck and Goldsmith (1984); Johnson and Scholes (1988); Peters and Waterman (1982)).[61]

'Organisational culture' has been variously described as 'the social glue that holds the organisation together' (Baker, 1980), 'a shared system or paradigm of belief and meaning' (Pfeffer, 1981), or quite simply 'how things are done around here' (Ouchi and Johnson, 1978). One of the fullest and most useful definitions is furnished by Edgar Schein: 'the deeper level of basic *assumptions and beliefs* that are shared by members of an organisation, that operate unconsciously and define in a basic "taken for granted" fashion an organisation's view of itself and its environment'.[62] And, as Peters and Waterman stress, this social glue which is so difficult to pin down is in fact extremely powerful indeed:

> Now, culture is the softest stuff around. Who trusts its leading analysts — anthropologists and sociologists — after all? Businessmen don't surely. Yet culture is the hardest stuff around, as well. Violate the lofty phrase, 'IBM Means Service', and you are out of a job, the company's security programme to the contrary notwithstanding. Digital is crazy (soft). Digital is anarchic (soft). 'People at Digital don't know who they work for', says a colleague. But they do know quality: the products they turn out work (hard). So 'Soft is hard'.[63]

Given this, it would seem to be a mistake to view the French and British water firms simply as inhabiting two separate camps. They are distinguished individually by such things as management quality and aggressiveness. But the stuff of their 'organisational culture', less easy to apprehend, also differentiates them; this includes their image, the extent to which that reflects a true corporate identity, and — in the case of the British firms — their ability to make a necessary culture jump.

It is the contention of this study that cultural specificities — in terms of both the cultural patterns which permeate the socio-political fabrics of Britain and France and the organisational culture of the various actors concerned — will play a significant role in influencing if not determining their respective performances in the years following privatisation and the dismantling of barriers within Europe.

Ultimately the singular contribution which the present study can make to the categories of research discussed above is perhaps this: as the very nature of the project implies, and as the report will attempt to demonstrate as it unfolds, these categories are not in fact mutually exclusive but overlapping. The unique contribution of this study therefore lies in its essentially interdisciplinary nature.

Notes

1. For a useful discussion of the issue prior to its resolution, see Woolcock, S. (1989), 'European Mergers: national or community controls?', *Royal Institute for International Affairs Discussion Paper Series*, no. 15.

2. On French attempts to install an EC-wide anti-trust system, see William Dawkins, 'French coax EC states toward entente on merger controls', *Financial Times*, 31 July 1989, p. 2.

3. See Butt Philip, A. (1988), 'Implementing the European Internal Market: problems and prospects', *Royal Institute for International Affairs Discussion Paper Series*, no. 5, and Siedentopf, H. and Ziller, J., eds. (1988), *Making European Policies Work: the implementation of Community legislation in the member states*, Sage, London.

4. House of Lords Select Committee on the European Communities (1989), *Nitrate in Water*, HL Paper 73; *Water Pollution from Farm Waste 1988: England and Wales* (1989), Water Authorities Association (WAA), Ministry of Agriculture, Fisheries and Food (MAFF).

5. A useful account of the cultural specificities of French business is offered by Barsoux, J.-L. and Lawrence, P. (1990), *Management in France*, Cassell, London. On the ways in which the French and British economies diverge, see in particular Hall, P. (1986), *Governing the Economy: the politics of state intervention in Britain and France*, Polity Press, Cambridge, and also Hayward, J. (1986), *The State and the Market Economy: industrial patriotism and economic intervention in France*, Wheatsheaf, Brighton.

6. Cited in Bateson, G. (1972), *Steps to an Ecology of Mind: collected essays in anthropology, psychiatry, evolution, and epistemology*, p. 459.

7. Sharp, M. and Shearman, C. (1987), *European Technological Collaboration*, Routledge and Kegan Paul, London, p. 90.

8. Personal interview with the author, November 1990, Paris.

9. See for example Jouve, E. (1967), *Le Général de Gaulle et la construction de l'Europe (1940–1946)*, Librairie Générale de Droit et de Jurisprudence, Paris.

10. Lord Cockfield's preface to *Europe Without Frontiers — completing the internal market*, (1987), Office for Official Publication of the European communities, European Documentation Series, no. 4, Luxembourg, opens with this citation.

11. For an incisive account of privatisation in Britain throughout the 1980s, see Chapman, C. (1990), *Selling the Family Silver: has privatization worked?*, Hutchinson Business Books, London.

12. On the French privatisation programme, see Bizaguet, A. (1988), *Le Secteur Public et les privatisations*, Presses Universitaires de France, Paris; de Belot, J. (1987), *Guide des privatisables*, Albin Michel, Paris; Maclean, M. (1987), 'The future of privatisation in France: a crisis of confidence?' *Modern and Contemporary France*, no. 31, pp. 1–9, and (1989), 'Privatisation and people's capitalism in France: old habits in new guises?' *Contemporary French Civilization*, vol. XIII, no. 1, pp. 1–18.

13. Bowers, J. et al. (1988), *Liquid Assets: the likely effects of privatisation of the water authorities on wildlife habitats and landscape*, Council for the Protection of Rural England (CPRE), Royal Society for the Protection of Birds (RSPB), World Wildlife Fund (WWF).

14. Rees, J. and Synnott, M. (1986), 'Are the Water Authorities an attractive prospect?' *Public Money*, pp. 46–51.

15. See 'A delicate case of jurisdictions', *Financial Times*, 20 September 1990.

16. This survey was conducted by management consultants Bain and Co. See their report, *La Stratégie des entreprises industrielles face à la demande mondiale*. For a résumé of their findings see 'Les grandes entreprises françaises sont trop petites', *La Tribune de l'Expansion*, 5 July 1989, p. 7, or 'Time to take the war to the enemy', *Financial Times*, 9 November 1989.

17. See Banque de France, *La Croissance externe des entreprises françaises à l'étranger*, August 1989, or 'Extérieures, toutes. . .', *Le Monde*, 4 October 1989, pp. 29, 44.

18. Cited in 'A delicate case of jurisdictions', op. cit.

19. For a useful discussion of the uncertainties which surround the new merger policy, see 'How conflict threatens to dog EC's new merger role', *The Times*, 1 August 1990, and 'Uncharted obstacle course towards one-stop control system', *Financial Times*, 21 September 1990.

20. Albert, M. and Ball, R. J. (1983), *Towards European economic recovery in the 1980s*, Report to the European Parliament.

21. See Cecchini, P. (1988), *The European Challenge: 1992 — the benefits of a Single Market*, Gower, London. (This study was commissioned by the EC.)

22. While consumption has continued to rise, it has still to reach the levels of other European nations: in 1984, for example, the French drank a litre per head per week, and the British a litre per head per year. CECG, op. cit., p. 1.

23. Reported in 'Mineral water sales soar', *Financial Times*, 30 May 1989, p. 13.

24. See 'Troubled Waters', *The Economist*, 16 September 1989, p. 41.

25. The EC has been concerned with protecting the environment since its inception; yet there has been some debate as to whether the environmental legislation of the Treaty of Rome (1957) was congruent with other provisions of the treaty. The amendment of the treaty in 1987 by the Single European Act (SEA) has given a clear basis for legal actions by the Community relating to the environment: henceforth, measures for protecting the environment shall be fully integrated with the Community's other policies. (See Article 130R(2) of the SEA.) On the infringement of EC legislation by member states, see *The Fifth Annual Report to the European Parliament on Commission monitoring of the application of Community law* (1987), COM (88) 425, 3 October 1988.

26. The EC directives on water embrace the following: detergents; surface water for drinking; sampling surface water for drinking; drinking water; water standards for freshwater fish; shellfish waters; bathing water; dangerous substances in water; groundwater; mercury from chloralkali industry; mercury from other sources; cadmium; lindane; DDT, carbon tetrachloride and pentachlorophenol; titanium dioxide; oil pollution at sea; and exchange of information on water.

27. Haigh, N., op. cit, p. 6.

28. See 'Britain in hot water with Commission, *Financial Times*, 8 February 1989, p. 2. Under the relevant article of the Treaty of Rome, the Commission sends a formal notice letter to the offending state, follows this up with a 'reasoned opinion' which clarifies the Commission's interpretation of EC law, and only goes to the European Court of Justice as a last resort.

29. Bowers et al., op. cit., p. 43. On the introduction of bias into objective setting where feedforward control is lacking, see Otley, D. (1987), *Accounting Control and Organizational Behaviour*, Heinemann, London, pp. 54–7.

30. Haigh, N., op. cit., p. 22.

31. Personal interview with the author, June 1989.

32. Cited in Rose, C., op. cit., p. 30.

33. See for example *Single Market News*, nos. 1–4, or publications from the DTI's *Europe open for Business* series.

34. Butt Philip, A. (1988), op. cit., p. 1.

35. See 'Poll shows British want integration in Europe', *Facts*, July 1989, p. 1.

36. Backing Mrs Thatcher were the Bruges group, named after her attack on a federal Europe delivered in Bruges in September 1988, and later (and more ignobly), the editor of the *Sun*, who ran a vulgar front-page, anti-Delors campaign throughout the month of November 1990.

37. A brief extract from Sir Geoffrey Howe's resignation speech to the House of Commons on 13 November 1990.

38. See Holcblat, N. and Tavernier, J.-L. (1989), 'Entre 1979 et 1986, la France a perdu des parts de marché industriel', *Economie et Statistique*, nos. 217–8, pp. 37–49.

39. See Hoffmann, S. (1987). 'France and Europe: the dichotomy of autonomy and cooperation', in Howorth, J. and Ross, G. (1987), *Contemporary France: a review of interdisciplinary studies*, vol. 1., Pinter, London, pp. 49–50.

40. President Mitterrand repeated this remark in his speech to the Royal Institute of International Affairs at Chatham House, London, on 15 January 1987.

41. Delors, J. and Clisthène (1988), *La France par l'Europe*, Grasset, Paris.

42. A leitmotif used by President Mitterrand (at the time of the postponement of the completion of the Chunnel rail link) to depict Britain's position within Europe, particularly in relation to the combined 'driving force' of France and the former West Germany. Lord Cockfield used a similar metaphor: Britain, he claimed, was always 'missing the bus'.

43. Hayward, J. (1976), 'Institutional inertia and political impetus in France and Britain', *European Journal of Political Research*, no. 4, p. 341.

44. Hall, P., op. cit., p. 283.

45. Cited in Lane, C. (1989), *Management and Labour in Europe*, Edward Elgar, Aldershot, p. 294.

46. The classic study by sociologist Geert Hofstede identifying core dimensions of culture as shown by Shell personnel throughout the world, presented the

French people as — amongst other things — having a powerful need to avoid uncertainty, and hence as strongly risk-averse. See Hofstede, G. (1980), *Culture's Consequences*, Sage, London.

47. Berger, S. (1987), 'Liberalism Reborn: the new liberal synthesis in France', in Howorth, J. and Ross, G., op. cit., pp. 84–108.

48. Cited in Servan-Schreiber, J.-L. (1990), *Le Métier de patron*, Fayard, Paris, p. 13.

49. Televised address to the French nation, 15 January 1984. Cited in the introduction to Machin, H. and Wright, V., eds. (1985), *Economic Policy and Policy-Making under the Mitterrand Presidency 1981–1984*, Pinter, London, p. 3.

50. P.G. Cerny refers to this new role for the state as one of 'tactical' or 'arm's length' *dirigisme*. See Cerny, P. G. (1989) 'From *Dirigisme* to Deregulation? The case of financial markets', in Godt, P., ed., *Policy-Making in France*, Pinter, London, p. 158.

51. 'The political culture of a society consists of the system of empirical beliefs, expressive symbols, and values which defines the situation in which political action takes place. It provides the subjective orientation to politics'. Cited in Verba, S. (1965), 'Comparative political culture', in Pye, L. and Verba S. (eds.), *Political Culture and Political Development*, Princeton University Press, Princeton, p. 513.

52. The 'dereliction of the water industry' is discussed in 'A decade of privatisation', *Financial Times*, 14 August 1989, p. 10.

53. Rees, J. and Synnott, M., op. cit., p. 51.

54. I am grateful to Sir Frederick Corfield for forwarding me a copy of this letter, dated 12 March 1986.

55. UBS Phillips and Drew, op. cit., p. 80.

56. RPI + K is the formula to be used for price changes in the industry. Thus, each year prices will increase by a percentage which reflects the retail price index for the previous year plus 'K', a figure agreed by government and the individual water authorities and companies, to be enforced for a maximum of ten years, and renegotiable after five. This K factor therefore includes all known obligations which are costable: the EC drinking water directives (apart from pesticides, mains); the EC bathing water directive; mains and sewerage asset management plans; current storm overflow and sea outfall consents; and nutrient reduction in eutrophic areas. But there are known obligations which are uncosted, and of course obligations which are as yet unknown. See UBS Phillips and Drew, op. cit., p. 59. These K factors range from just 3 per cent for Yorkshire to 7 per cent for Northumbrian, with whom it lies to clean up Blackpool beach, at an estimated cost of £50 million.

57. Bowers, J. et al. (1989), *Liquid Costs*, op. cit., p. 11.

58. UBS Phillips and Drew, op. cit., p. 58.

59. See also Bowers, J. and O'Donnell, K. (1987), 'Privatisation and the Control of Pollution', *University of Leeds School of Business and Economic Studies Discussion Paper Series*, no. 87/10, and Bowers, J. et al. (1988), 'Privatisation of the water supply: some outstanding issues', *University of Leeds School of Economic Studies Discussion Paper Series*.

60. Johnson, G. and Scholes, K. (1988), *Exploring Corporate Strategy*, Prentice Hall, London, p. 37.

61. Clutterbuck, D. and Goldsmith, W. (1984), *The Winning Streak*, Weidenfeld and Nicolson, London, and Peters, T. J. and Waterman, R. H. (1982), *In Search of Excellence*, Harper and Row, New York. The citation is from Johnson and Scholes, op. cit., p. 38.

62. Schein, E. (1985), *Organisational Culture and Leadership*, Jossey Bass, London, p. 6.

63. Peters, T. J. and Waterman, R. H., op. cit., p. 319.

. . . , . . . , . . . , . . . , . . . , . . . , ...

. . . .

3 The Water Industry in England and Wales: historical sources and political springs

Water, water every where,
Nor any drop to drink   — (Coleridge).

A historical perspective: the water industry in England and Wales, 1900–89

Prior to the 1973 Water Act, which incorporated the various branches of the water industry into ten regional water authorities, numerous bodies were responsible for the three separate services provided by the water industry: water supply, sewerage services and river functions.

Water supply

At the turn of the century, the industry was fragmented and variegated: as many as 2,000 individual water suppliers were operating in England and Wales alone.[1] Some were private companies or local authority waterworks constituted by private Acts of Parliament; others were local authority waterworks operating under Public Health Acts enacted in the last century; others still were joint water boards comprising two or more local authority undertakings. Common to all, however, was the monopoly which each had in its own area.

With the 1945 Water Act,[2] all relevant legislation was recodified into one standard 'Waterworks Code', many of whose provisions — such as the obligation to supply, the compulsory acquisition of land and water rights, the breaking open of streets — were restated in 1973 and still apply to this day. The 1945 Act sought to promote industry efficiency, to which end it encouraged the amalgamation of water undertakers. Thus, the 1,400 suppliers operating in the 1940s in England and Wales became 950 by 1950, 276 by 1968, and as few as 187 immediately prior to the 1974 reorganisation of water management which succeeded the 1973 Act.[3] Twenty-nine private companies slipped through the net of this last act of rationalisation: these are the statutory water companies which, until their recent changes in ownership, had survived reorganisation and new legislation largely intact.[4]

Sewerage services

Statutory control of sewerage services has been in place in England and Wales since the fifteenth century.[5] Prior to industrialisation, it was customary for 'night soil' to be taken from latrines in the towns and distributed to nearby market gardens. The trebling of the population in the first half of the nineteenth century, however, put a stop to this practice, replacing it with tens of thousands of cesspools. But water from cesspools seeped into drinking water wells; cholera was the result. In 1832 it claimed the lives of 5,000 Londoners, precipitating the 1848 City Sewers Act, by which the connection of all London homes to drains and the use of flush water closets became compulsory.[6] That same year, however, 53,000 died of the disease nationwide.

Nevertheless there was, until 1973, little impetus to *rationalise* the sewerage services of England and Wales. The economic and health problems associated with transporting sewage over long distances (the need for stormwater flows, the danger to public health should sewage turn septic), together with the widespread availability of rivers for the discharge of effluent, had meant the preservation into the 1970s of some 1,400 bodies responsible for serving small local areas.[7] These were governed by Public Health Acts dating from the nineteenth century (1848, 1872, 1875), and in particular by the Public Health Act of 1936. In 1973, however, their numbers were cut at one fell swoop to a mere ten: the ten water authorities of England and Wales.

River functions

The 1948 River Boards Act saw the creation of 32 river boards, each based on the catchment area for a river or confluent of rivers, to be responsible for pollution control, land drainage and fisheries. The 1951 Rivers (Prevention of Pollution) Act set out to reinforce the first of these functions. But its objective to 'maintain and restore the wholesomeness of rivers and other inland and coastal waters'[8] was countermanded by the permission or 'consent' which the boards were authorised to give for notionally 'illegal' substances to be discharged into rivers. Later, with the rising demand for water from industry and agriculture which characterised the 1950s and 1960s, the coordination of resource planning was found to be wanting, ushering in the 1963 Water Resources Act. This reduced the number of river boards to 27 River Authorities, which, together with the Thames Conservancy and Lee Conservancy Catchment Boards, henceforth covered England and Wales. Once again, however, the Act succeeded only partially, as the river authorities, bowing to government pressure to curb public spending, continued to turn a blind eye to the infringement of discharge consents by local authorities

—an early indication of the need, which has only recently been publicly recognised, for an independent regulatory body.

This process of industry concentration, which rationalised each of the core activities separately, culminated in the Water Act of 1973. In the drive towards centralisation which typified the early 1970s, and which saw the abolition of the shires in favour of larger regions, the three arms of the industry were united. The implementation of the Act in 1974 saw the dismantlement of the 29 river authorities and boards and their replacement by ten all-purpose, regional water authorities, to be responsible for the management of almost all aspects of the water cycle—including its recreational use—in each of their areas. The Act represented a major shift to integrated river basin management, and established a regional forum for decision making. Public cries for stricter pollution control were heard, and partial regulation ceded to self-regulation; although whether this was the best form of regulatory regime is clearly open to question. As a system it was certainly open to abuse. The authorities themselves were dominated by local government officials and industrialists. And as Chris Rose pertinently remarks, 'Viewed with the rosiest spectacles available, and with the greatest possible faith in human nature, it is impossible to avoid the conclusion that these gentlemen, with such backgrounds and interests, would be likely to err in favour of acceding to industrial demands rather than upholding tighter environmental standards'.[9]

From 1973 onwards, until the privatisation of the industry in December 1989, the structure and responsibilities of the water industry were as given in Table 3.1. Unusually, the above legislation—which resulted in an industry which was partly nationalised (77 per cent), partly in private hands (23 per cent)—was enacted under the auspices of a Conservative government, headed by Edward Heath. Truer to its political origins was the 1977 Water Charges Equalisation Act, Labour legislation which provided for the evening out among water authorities of the costs incurred by them for the supply of unmeasured water, in striking contrast to the French system which maintains that one must pay for what one consumes. Nevertheless, the 1980s were characterised by a growing belief in *accountability*. In particular, there was a growing feeling that prices should be seen to reflect costs, at individual customer levels. Water authorities first attempted to introduce metering in 1981, but there was little take-up from existing customers. As a result, many authorities adopted a policy of metering all new houses in their area.

Similarly, the 1983 Water Act, which introduced a more professional managerial approach to the board and excluded local government membership from it, was indicative both of the entrepreneurial thrust of the Thatcher decade and of her well-documented battle against local councils.[10] With the 1983 Act, the National Water Council, an advisory body to the industry established ten years previously, was renamed the Water Authorities Asso-

ciation. It was also at this time that the dilapidation of the sewerage system was becoming more noticeable, particularly in northern urban centres.
While the common British attitude to this alarmingly invisible industry has
tended to be, as one journalist put it, 'flush and forget',[11] industrial disloca-
tion and traffic diversions caused by flooding due to structural deterioration
proved to be very tangible problems indeed. In 1987 a Commons Environment Committee conceded that 1,000 crumbling sewers in the North West
Water region alone, and as many as 5,000 throughout England and Wales,
were urgently in need of replacement.

Table 3.1

Structure of the Water Industry 1973–89		
Accountability	Responsible Body	Service
Shareholders (Statutory Control of Dividends and Reserves)	Water Companies	Water Supply
DoE (Financial Performance)	Water Authorities	Pollution Control Recreation Resource Planning Sewerage Services Water Supply
MAFF (Financial Performance)	Water Authorities	Land Drainage
Adapted from: UBS Phillips and Drew (1989) *The Water Industry in England and Wales*		

A political perspective: privatisation and the changing economic landscape

'Tis not enough to help the feeble up, but to support him after
— (Shakespeare).

Over the last decade, governments of different political persuasions in countries of different stages of development and for a whole host of different
reasons have been questioning the role of the state in the economy. With
the widespread and increasing indebtedness and international monetary in-
stability which characterised the 1980s, governments of many guises have
turned to the public sector as a major source of savings, and in this the
International Monetary Fund (IMF) has emerged as an unexpected motor,
often making financial aid dependent upon structural change. Even com-

munist regimes have begun to court foreign private companies and investment, which some have called 'hidden privatisation'. By December 1989 as
many as 800 joint ventures had been set up in the Soviet Union alone with
the participation of private firms from OECD countries (Organisation for
Economic Cooperation and Development).[12] But in this 'worldwide dash
to privatisation' (Fraser, 1988), it is without any doubt the United King-
dom which emerged as the front runner.[13] For here, at breakneck speed,
a decade of denationalisation transferred to private hands public assets to
the value of £27 billion. If this pace were to be maintained — and the new
man at no. 10, John Major, insisted in his 1991 New Year message to the
nation that it would be — the proceeds from privatisation are expected to
reach one-fifth of the present national debt by the year 1992, and sweeping and irreversible change in Britain's economic landscape will have been
achieved.[14]

It became apparent almost as soon as Margaret Thatcher had moved into
Downing Street that a new relationship between government and industry was about to be brought into play. It also became apparent that Mrs
Thatcher was a very *particular* type of prime minister. Determined to exercise a decisive influence over her party and the tightest of controls over
her Cabinet, she had her finger in almost every pie — except where being
seen to be at one remove from an unpopular policy or event was electorally
desirable, as when Ian MacGregor was appointed chairman of another nationalised industry — coal — to lead the attack on 'the enemy within' during
the 1984-85 miners' strike.[15]

Tight control can be useful, in that it helps to promote coherence of action.
If the benefit of any control is derived from an increase in the likelihood that
organisational goals will be achieved, then, as Merchant (1985) suggests,
tight control is good because it provides a high degree of certainty that
people will act as desired.[16] But, Peters and Waterman (1982) insist, it is
only good with 'plenty of rope' — autonomy and the freedom to perform
— for the rank and file.[17] Otherwise innovation and imagination are stifled;
and harmful side effects result from the cause-effect relationship triggered
by the control mechanism (Stout, 1980).[18]

But government is far from being a typical organisation. *Cabinet* government, moreover, is one of the key pillars in the complex edifice of British
democracy. Its effective eclipse for more then eleven years — which, in
the end, doubtless contributed to the former prime minister's demise in
November 1990, when the right to Cabinet government was once again re-
asserted — allowed Mrs Thatcher to go a long way towards fashioning a
nation which was very much in her own image.[19]

Privatisation, or denationalisation, which Mrs Thatcher's biographer
Hugo Young terms 'the most sacred of Tory obsessions',[20] was not, however, the brain-child of Margaret Thatcher despite her close association
with the policy. As a political theory it was first given substance in Peter

Drucker's seminal work *The Age of Discontinuity: guidelines to our changing society* (1969). Here Drucker argued that government should be responsible solely for *strategy*, for decision and direction, and that it should have the strength — and sense — to leave the *doing* to others. This belief in the limits of government was one which Mrs Thatcher whole-heartedly embraced. For her, the monopoly nationalised companies represented a problem as great as that posed by the trade union grip on British industry.

Embryonic plans for the extensive privatisation of Britain's nationalised companies and industries — although initially the use of the word 'privatisation' was studiously avoided lest electorate sensibilities be offended — began to emerge in the early months and years of Thatcher's premiership. By 1982, a multi-purpose rationale for privatisation had crystallised. In September of that year Energy Secretary Nigel Lawson clarified the government's viewpoint: 'No industry should remain under state ownership unless there is a positive and overwhelming case for it so doing. Inertia is not good enough. We simply cannot afford it'.[21]

The political hopes invested in privatisation were considerable, for it was designed at once:

— to stimulate the economy;

— to subject state-owned monopolies to the full commercial discipline of the customer, within a new regulatory framework;

— to furnish financial resources and thus reduce public borrowing;

— to facilitate the expansion of share ownership (with its attendant political benefits for the Conservatives: privatisation is arguably a most useful proselytic weapon for any right-wing government, in that it is believed to successfully alter political allegiances);[22]

— to bring about 'the first post-socialist society'.[23]

The above rationale rests on a deep-seated belief in the innate superiority of private enterprise to public ownership, even in a situation of natural monopoly. For private ownership, it is said, leads to allocative and technical efficiency. That is, private industry delivers goods and services to the consumer at lower prices and/or higher quality, and produces these at lower cost and with a higher rate of productivity than is achievable in the public sector.[24] Ultimately, according to Roy Watts, chairman of Thames Water, it is all due to culture and style: 'The private sector is more efficient than the public sector. It is about style, about culture, about managerial freedom, about clarity, about accountability'.[25] Ian MacGregor explains this point more fully, equating nationalisation with administration and privatisation with management:

Nationalized industries were created by well-meaning people, but are, in the main, inefficient, overmanned and heavily dependent on public funds.

Mrs Thatcher has been right to seek to make them more responsive and efficient and to seek to keep them that way by privatizing them. Even a good socialist like President Mitterrand of France now wants to turn many of his nationalized industries back to private ownership.[26] Administration is the perpetuation of the existing system and the status quo. It is the essence of management to change and to improve things; management has to seek efficiency, identify the need for change and have the will to effect it. Administrators, by their nature, do not make changes.[27]

The conclusion drawn by the authors of what has been termed 'the most detailed analysis of privatisation in Britain to date' was, precisely, that the primary benefit of privatisation lies in its ability to successfully change the business culture of Britain (Bishop and Kay, 1988).[28] As Colin Chapman writes, if little change in management style was apparent in many of Britain's privatised organisations in the years following their change of status, in others nothing short of a 'cultural revolution' had taken place.[29]

A further advantage which has been claimed for privatisation is that it has thrown open the windows on industries which have long been shuttered from view, cocooned by their own bureaucracy.[30] When a window was opened on the water industry, its 'cracked pipes and Victorian sewerage systems'[31] — what has been called 'the dereliction of Britain's water industry'[32] — came under public scrutiny for the first time.

The muddy waters of privatisation

That the privatisation of water was not attempted until the sale of many other companies and industries had been successfully effected,[33] and further, that five long years intervened between the point of its proposal and the point of its accomplishment, are indicative of the 'muddy waters' which characterised the sale (see above, Chapter 1). Table 3.2 (below) traces its long course from conception to reality.

Table 3.2

Water Privatisation: Calendar of Events: 1985–89	
February 1985:	The Minister of State for the Environment announces during a debate on the water authorities (return on assets) that the government 'will be examining the possibility of a measure of privatisation in the industry'.

Table 3.2 (cont.)

Water Privatisation: Calendar of Events: 1985–89	
April 1985:	A discussion paper is sent to the chairmen of RWAs by the Minister for Housing and Construction (Ian Gow) on the implications of the possible introduction of a measure of privatisation into the water industry. The chairmen endorse Roy Watts' (chairman of Thames Water) recommendation that the concept of integrated river management be maintained.
February 1986:	Publication of the government White Paper 'Privatisation of the Water Industry in England and Wales' (Cmnd. 9734), which advocates that the industry be sold off as it stands, with only the functions of flood protection and land drainage retained in the public sector.
March 1986:	Consultation paper on Water and Sewerage Law.
April 1986:	Consultation paper on 'The Water Environment: the next steps'.
June 1986:	In response to lobbying from organisations such as the Confederation of British Industry (CBI) and the Country Landowners Association (CLA) — alarmed that control of environmental and regulatory matters would be retained by privatised companies, and insistent that 'poachers' should not also be 'gamekeepers' — Environment Secretary Nicholas Ridley postpones water privatisation plans.
July 1987:	Consultation paper on 'the National Rivers Authority — proposals'.
October 1987:	The greatest stock market crash in history occurs. Many small investors get their fingers burnt in the ill-timed sale of British Petroleum.
December 1987:	Government statement issued on 'the National Rivers Authority — policy'.
May 1988:	Public Utility Transfers and Water Charges Act 1988 receives Royal Assent. RWAs may proceed with restructuring in preparation for privatisation.
June 1988:	Water Authority restructuring commences.
November 1988:	Publication and first reading of the Water Bill.
December 1988:	Second reading of the Water Bill.

Table 3.2 (cont.)

Water Privatisation: Calendar of Events: 1985–89

January 1989:	Suddenly conscious that 13 per cent of the industry is in French hands, the government belatedly unveils a 'golden share' plan to protect the water authorities from unwelcome takeover for a five-year period from flotation (with the exception of Welsh Water, in which the government's share is to be held indefinitely). Shareholdings by any particular group are to be restricted to 15 per cent. It is simultaneously disclosed that water company takeovers with combined assets of more than £30 million will be monitored.
July 1989:	The Water Bill completes its passage through Parliament, and the 1989 Water Act receives Royal Assent.
September 1989:	On vesting day, the activities of the ten water authorities are divided into two. Responsibility for land drainage, water management, fisheries and navigation is transferred to the National Rivers Authority, the environmental regulator chaired by Lord Crickhowell. Responsibility for the economic regulation of the water and sewage businesses passes to the new Director General of Water Services (Ian Byatt), supported by an Office of Water Services: 'Ofwat'.
	The core utility functions of the ten RWAs are transferred to ten 'successor companies' set up by the Companies Act. The Government holds 100 per cent of the shares in the new public limited companies (e.g. Wessex Water plc), who, in turn, hold all the shares in the successor companies (e.g. Wessex Water Utilities Ltd.).
November 1989:	The price of the offer is disclosed (240p per share, to be paid in three instalments), and the final prospectus is published. The sale commences.
December 1989:	Close of sale. The government ceases to be the ultimate owner of the industry. The selling of water may well have proved to be a tricky task indeed, but the *sale itself* is an overwhelming success: the offer is found to be more than four times over-subscribed, as applications for 2.86 billion shares chase the 520 million available. Dealings commence.

Compiled by the author on the basis of information given in the *Financial Times* and Bowers et al. (1988), *Liquid Assets: the likely effects of privatisation of the water authorities on wildlife habitats and landscape.*

In February 1986, the government's White Paper on the privatisation of water had specified no fewer than eleven advantages which would accrue to the industry, its customers and employees, and even to 'the nation as a whole', as a result of its transfer to private ownership.[34] These were as follows:

1. Authorities would be free of ministerial intervention in day-to-day management and sheltered from the swing of the political pendulum.
2. They would at the same time be released from the financial constraints of the public expenditure budget.
3. Investment strategies would benefit from access to capital markets.
4. Comparison between authorities would be facilitated, enabling their relative efficiencies to be measured (the notion of 'comparative competition' discussed above, see Introduction).
5. Economic regulation would ensure that the benefits of greater efficiency were enjoyed by customers in the form of lower prices and improved services.
6. The water environment would be protected by a clearer strategic framework.
7. There would be a greater incentive to tailor services and tariffs to customer needs and preferences.
8. Greater competition would arise in the provision of various commercial services, such as consultancy abroad.
9. Privatised authorities would be better able to attract high quality management.
10. There would be the opportunity for wide share ownership among local customers and employees.
11. Employee motivation would improve accordingly.[35]

Yet if these alleged improvements were so indispensable, why then was there little but praise in the February 1986 White Paper for the achievements of the water industry under its existing structure? — praise which the following extract from a section which was later withdrawn (perhaps because such explicit commendation undermined the argument for change) amply exemplifies: 'The catchment-based structure of the water industry has worked well in practice. It has been recognised throughout the world as being a good and cost-effective model for other countries to follow'.[36] Praise which, according to Daniel A. Okun, was well deserved:

> The regional water authorities provide the highest quality of water supply and sewerage service to the largest percent of population, at the lowest cost of any water industry in any country in the world. This observer has

difficulty in understanding why, after only twelve years of operation, a
system which has steadily improved the quality of its service and reduced
the size of staff necessary to assure this service needs to be replaced by a
system which is unproven and gives promise of introducing major difficulties of implementation, inevitably impairing the quality of service and
most likely increasing the cost to those served.[37]

Perhaps one reason for government praise for the industry lay in the fact
that it provided a convenient excuse for political inertia; for the government intended to sell the water authorities essentially as they stood (see
above, Table 3.2). In the event, significant changes — particularly to the
proposed regulatory framework — proved necessary.

For however unequivocal the government may have felt the above 'advantages' to be, its attempt to sell its policy to the public at large was
generally seen as a failure,[38] despite the last-minute popularity of the sale
prompted by the low share price.[39] Labour threats to renationalise the industry at below the issue price did not help Conservatives in their efforts
to cajole a disaffected public. (Some time after the sale, with Labour's
prospects for electoral victory looking brighter than for many years amid
doubts concerning the leadership qualities of Mrs Thatcher's successor, such
threats have not diminished.) The government sustained huge losses of
£1.4 billion on the sale alone.[40] This does not include the cost to the ten
water plcs of flotation, estimated to total some £62 million.[41]

Nor does it include underwriting fees, calculated at £44.8 million.[42] Nor
the cost of an extensive three-month promotional campaign, priced at
£21 million, after which — 'after all the public relations hype, the months of
water commercials and the endless dribble of small announcements on the
privatisation of the water industry'[43] — the sale itself came as something of
an anti-climax. Added together, the above expenses come to £1.53 billion.
If the cost of the £5 billion debt write-off and a 'green dowry' worth £1.6 billion are included, the grand total of taxpayers' money spent on ensuring
that water privatisation was a political success amounts to a staggering
£8.3 billion. For what returns to the taxpayer? As *Financial Times* columnist
Lex wrote at the time, 'Chief dupe looks like being the taxpayer, who will
net only around £500 million as first payment on an industry which had
assets of £7.7 billion even on a limited historic accounting basis'.[44]

Why had the government consistently failed to convince the public of
the virtues of water privatisation when privatisation has generally been
so well received?[45] Why were 'barrow boy' tactics of perks, discounts and
underpriced shares necessary to ensure that the sell-off was not a flop?[46]

It seems that the government may have underestimated public anxieties
aroused by the water sale. Anxieties which concerned environmental protection and the cleanliness of our drinking water, beaches and rivers; for
water 'is a public good, [and] there are no markets in which environmental

quality is traded'.[47] Anxieties about price rises, and the effect of grafting a profit motive on to a vital industry, where customers are captive to one supplier. Anxieties about takeover protection, fuelled by the unwelcome efforts of three French groups to buy a piece of the action before the market woke up to the possibility of a leap in tariffs.

But above all else, the government seems to have underestimated public alarm concerning the regulation of the industry. In the words of one financial journalist, 'the Government is once again setting off in hot pursuit of Sid's cash without completing its strategy to protect the rest of us from monopoly abuse'.[48]

A watertight regulatory framework?

Given the strong monopoly power of the water industry, a formidable regulatory regime was crucial in order to protect the customer from monopoly abuse following its privatisation. Perhaps because the environmental and economic regulation of the industry had always been the weakest point in the government's proposal (leading to its postponement in June 1986, its amendment in January 1989, and to lengthy negotiations with water leaders), powerful regulation did indeed seem to have been provided.

A veritable regulatory army has been mustered, apparently designed to allay every fear. Environmental protection is now in the hands of a 6,000-strong National Rivers Authority,[49] while the overseeing of prices and quality of service falls to the 100-strong Office of Water Services (Ofwat), headed by the Director General of Water Services, currently Ian Byatt. As if that was not enough, a new Drinking Water Inspectorate was launched by the former Environment Secretary, Chris Patten, in January 1990, for the purpose of ensuring that drinking water did indeed comply with EC quality regulations (although in some cases even more rigorous standards were exacted). Meanwhile, breathing down the necks of water managers are also Her Majesty's Inspectorate of Pollution (HMIP), the Monopolies and Mergers Commission, and various local and regional Customer Services Committees (CSCs). Inept management is further threatened by the 'stick' of the capital market. And ultimately, there is the protection afforded by the European Community, with its umpteen directives on water, *more than for any other aspect of the environment*, and others — including one on wastewater — in the offing. The Commission also has authority over all mergers and acquisitions in the Community, where the global turnover of the companies concerned exceeds Ecu 5 billion, or where their combined turnover within the EC is greater than Ecu 250 million (see above, Chapter 2). But is all of this sufficient?

It is too soon, perhaps, to judge the success of this latest and most contentious phase in the government's grand strategy of privatisation: the sale

of large public sector monopolies. Nevertheless, it is legitimate to suggest —
as the Organisation for Economic Cooperation and Development suggested
in August 1989 — that the early part of the campaign was successful because
the companies concerned, companies like Britoil and Rolls-Royce, *belonged
naturally in the private sector.*[50] Industries like water, gas and telecommunications, on the other hand, *clearly escape normal competition.* But the implications of unleashing a profit motive on all three are far more serious
in the case of water: for water is essential to life. And, as the OECD has
warned, a bad utility management may even be more secure in the private
sector, cushioned from harsh reality by a dispersed and passive sharehold-
ing body, and sheltered from predators by protective 'golden shares'. In
January 1991, South West Water was found guilty of supplying foul-tasting,
heavily polluted drinking water to 20,000 consumers in the Camelford area
of North Cornwall in July 1988 (having repeatedly reassured them that the
water, laced with aluminium sulphate, was fit to drink), and fined £10,000
accordingly.[51] Yet the company's share value barely reacted to the news, and
its management team was preserved intact. With water shares perceived
as quasi-gilt-edged securities, and shareholders shielded from unforeseen
expenditure through the protective mechanism of 'cost pass-through', it is
perhaps not surprising.

How, moreover, is the Janus-faced Director General of Water Services to
conciliate the conflicting demands of customers and shareholders, to whom
he is equally responsible? Perhaps only through being a hands-off, arm's
length regulator, as Ian Byatt has indeed promised to be.[52] But without a
hands-on, vigilant regulator, how is customer protection from monopoly
exploitation to be assured? Not that shareholders are to have it all their
own way. At the moment, shareholders are 'making hay while the sun
shines': in the year following the privatisation of the industry, with the
effects of the recession beginning to bite, and company profits dented by
high interest rates, water shares outperformed the market by an average of
34 per cent. Nevertheless, with Labour threats to renationalise the industry,
a residual political risk remains. And according to financial journalists, the
considerable underperformance of British Gas and British Telecom shares
in recent years resulted more from regulatory uncertainties than from any
fundamental weakness in their underlying businesses.[53]

With the advent of the NRA, poacher is clearly no longer playing gamekeeper. But the authority is as yet untried. How action-oriented will it
prove? Might not its large numbers lead directly to another administration of the kind described above by Ian MacGregor — to another creeping
bureaucracy?[54] There is little fear of that being allowed to happen. One year
after its launch, the NRA was already beginning to be perceived — certainly
through no fault of its own — as short-staffed, underpowered, and saddled
with the impossible task of implementing environmental improvement in
a financial strait-jacket.[55]

Meanwhile, the EC may well have agreed its new merger policy. However, as few as 50 mergers per year are likely to have the necessary combined turnover to qualify for EC vetting. And the acquisitions with which we are concerned here would indubitably be among the many others which would slip through the loose mesh of its over-generous net.

Ultimately, protection for the management of the new water companies — that is, if they are unable to protect themselves — rests with the government's five-year golden share, when foreign holdings are to be restricted to 15 per cent. The golden share is expected to be retained for a further five years (1994–99), during which time higher levels of foreign ownership may be permitted.

Foreign investors need not be unduly perturbed. They may not have to wait so long. However garrisoned the water plcs may appear to be, the unforeseen waiving of the government's golden share in Jaguar in November 1989, and its equally sudden purchase by the American car maker, Ford, have shown to all and sundry that, in the last analysis, the government's regulatory armour is — perhaps by design? — by no means invincible.

Notes

1. See report by UBS Phillips and Drew, op. cit., pp. 9–12.

2. Separate legislation was enacted in the mid- to late 1940s regarding Scotland and Northern Ireland.

3. These 187 water undertakers comprised: 100 water boards, 57 local authority undertakings and 30 private companies.

4. This was partly because government had recognised that all water suppliers were not in a position to apply the 1945 Act to the letter. It was therefore acceptable to vary the terms of the Act by Ministerial Order. As a result, prior to the 1974 reorganisation, some water suppliers had applied the Act fully; others had applied it in tempered form; and others still — quite legitimately — had not applied it at all.

5. Corfield, The Rt. Hon. Sir F. V., op. cit.

6. For a fuller discussion of the evolution and development of statutory control of sewerage services, see Rose, C., op. cit., pp. 12–13

7. These 1,400 operators consisted of: 1,364 local authorities, 27 joint sewerage services, the City of London and the Greater London Council (GLC).

8. Cited in Rose, C., op. cit., p. 44.

9. ibid, p. 58.

10. Mrs Thatcher battled with local government in general and left-wing councils in particular. Her success can be judged from the fact that, as Hugo Young writes, 'The validity of local government as a function relevant to British democracy ceased to be taken for granted'. Cited in Young, H. (1989), *One of Us*, Pan Books/Macmillan, London, p. 538.

11. Evans, R., 'Privatisation: a bridge over troubled water', *Financial Times*, Supplement on Water, 25 November 1989, p. IX.

12. Reported in Martinet, G. (1990), '70 entrepreneurs confrontent leurs expériences à l'est', *Nouvelle Europe*, no. 2, June 1990, p. 55.

13. Fraser, R., op. cit., p. x.

14. Reported to be high on the government's privatisation agenda are the Export Credits Guarantee Department, the trust ports, the British Technology Group, the government's 48.8 per cent holding in British Telecom, the municipal airports, British Coal and the Post Office. See 'Full steam ahead for the big State sell-off', *Independent on Sunday*, 13 January 1991, pp. 4–5. The long-promised privatisation of British Rail, on the other hand, now looks less certain.

15. The epithet is Thatcher's own, used to describe militant miners during the strike, and contrasted with 'the enemy without' whom she had defeated during the Falklands campaign. MacGregor later used this as the title to his account of the strike. See MacGregor, I. with Tyler, R., (1987), *The Enemies Within: the story of the Miners' Strike, 1984–5*, Fontana/Collins, Glasgow, p. 172.

16. Merchant, K. (1985), *Control in Business Organizations*, p. 58.

17. Peters, T. J. and Waterman, R. H., op. cit., pp. 318–25.

18. Stout, R. (1980), *Management or Control?: the organizational challenge*, Indiana University Press, Bloomington, p. 4.

19. Scotland, however, categorically rejected the Thatcherite model.

20. Young, H., op. cit., p. 130.

21. ibid, p. 360.

22. Thatcher's privatisation programme has contained a strong proselytic element, epitomised by the British Gas campaign to 'tell Sid'; and it has been suggested that she was re-elected in 1983, and again in 1987, because she had sold off council houses and privatised British Telecom. While share-owning does not dislodge the class system, it may blur the boundaries by modifying the ways in which people perceive themselves.

23. Fraser, R., op. cit., p. ix.

24. Bowers, J. et al., (1988), op. cit., p. 8.

25. Cited in 'No need to muddy the water'. Letter addressed to the *Financial Times*, 11 February 1989, p. 7.

26. This is not strictly true: the French privatisation programme was introduced by right-wing Prime Minister Chirac, while left-wing President Mitterrand refused to sign the ordinance. But it is nevertheless noticeable that there have been no 'deprivatisations' since Chirac's demise in the presidential elections of April–May 1988 and the subsequent return of the socialists to government. Indeed, President Mitterrand promised at the time of his 1988 presidential election campaign that there would be no nationalisation of privatised companies.

27. MacGregor, I. with Tyler, R., op. cit., pp. 67–8.

28. Cited in 'Privatisation as an end in itself', *Financial Times*, 25 November 1988, p. 7. See Bishop, M. and Kay, J. (1988), *Does Privatisation Work? Lessons from the UK*, London Business School, London.

29. Chapman, C., op. cit., p. 105.

30. 'A decade of privatisation', op. cit.

31. See 'Regulatory gaps in water', *Financial Times*, 21 July 1988, p. 22.

32. 'A decade of privatisation', op. cit.

33. Previous privatisations, in order of offer for sale, include: British Petroleum Company Limited; Fairey; Ferranti; British Aerospace plc; Cable and Wireless plc; Amersham International plc; National Freight Company; Britoil plc; Associated British Ports Holdings plc; British Rail Hotels; International Aeradio; British Gas—Wytch Farm; Enterprise Oil plc; Jaguar plc; Sealink UK Limited; Inmos; British Telecommunications plc; Brooke Marine Limited; Yarrow Shipbuilders Limited; Vosper Thorneycroft Limited; Swan Hunter Shipbuilders Limited; Hall Russell Limited; Vickers Shipbuilding and Engineering Limited; BA Helicopters; British Gas plc; National Bus Company; Leyland Bus; British Airways plc; Royal Ordnance; British Leyland Trucks; Rolls-Royce plc; DAB; Istel; BAA plc; British Steel. Sources: Price Waterhouse (1987), *Privatisation: the facts*; *Financial Times*.

34. White Paper on 'the Privatisation of the Water Authorities in England and Wales' (Cmnd. 9734), para. 3.

35. White Paper, Cmnd. 9734, para. 3. These alleged advantages are assessed by Corfield, Sir F. V., op. cit.

36. White Paper, Cmnd. 9734, Section 4, paras. 30–5, later abandoned.

37. Okun, D. A., letter to the *Guardian*, op. cit.

38. See 'Water leaders agree that ministers failed to "sell" privatisation', *Financial Times*, 6 March 1989, p. 8.

39. According to Colin Chapman, there were three fundamental reasons for the ultimate success of the sale: the promotional campaign; the low share price; and the fact that the water companies were local concerns with which small investors could identify, yet which nevertheless offered a low-risk investment. See Chapman, C., op. cit., p. 49.

40. The share issue valued the industry at only £5.24 billion, which was £1.4 billion less than the sum of the debt which had been written off (£5 billion) and the government's so-called 'green dowry' (£1.6 billion) for environmental improvements. This was at the lower end of what the industry had been expected to fetch, estimated at between £5 billion and £7 billion.

41. See 'Water issue costing 10 companies £62m', *Financial Times*, 23 November 1989, p. 1.

42. The offer prospectus published on 22 November 1989 made this disclosure.

43. Cited in 'Water price fails to make a splash', *Financial Times*, 23 November 1989, p. 8.

44. Cited in Chapman, C., op. cit., p. 40.

45. See 'Consumers still fear water privatisation', op. cit.

46. It was thus that Gordon Brown, Labour's shadow minister for trade and industry, described the government's behaviour on the day of the sale.

47. Quoted in Bowers, J. et al. (1988), op. cit., p. 9.

48. 'If you see Sid, commiserate', *Financial Times*, 3 March 1989, p. 16.

49. The NRA's wide-ranging responsibilities include: the maintenance and improvement of the quality of inland, coastal and underground waters; control of pollution; the management of rivers and other water resources; the issuing of licenses to industry for water abstraction; land drainage and flood defence; the improvement and development of fisheries and navigation functions; and the provision of recreation amenities.

50. See 'A decade of privatisation', op. cit.

51. See 'Camelford victims criticise "low" fine on water authority', *Independent*, 9 July 1991.

52. 'Water watchdog in "arm's length" pledge', *Financial Times*, 9 August 1989, p. 6.

53. See, for example, 'The tricky task of selling water', *Financial Times*, 29 August 1989, p. 18.

54. Ironically, 6,000 was the original figure suggested by water chiefs, and rejected as scaremongering by Nicholas Ridley, former Secretary of State for the En-

vironment. See 'Water industry surprised by strict regulation plan', *Financial Times*, 21 November 1988, p. 6.

55. See 'Swift currents below the surface', *Financial Times*, 14 December 1990, p. 16.

4 The French Invasion: the reasons why, the grounds for caution

Put five rats in a cage and what do they do?
They try to get out of the cage
— (Olivier Celier, International Development Manager of SAUR).

A Gallic toe in British waters

The French came quietly in 1987, stealthily stalking an unknown prey in an unknown sector of an unknown industry: Britain's 28 remaining statutory water companies, the minnows which had slipped through the net of repeated rationalisations.

For years there had been little movement in the ownership of the shares of Britain's private water companies. They were small fry, with a low yield, their 1988 aggregate pre-tax profits being lower than that of the smallest water authority. Small fry they may have appeared, but they nevertheless allowed three French water companies to build themselves a Trojan horse under the very noses of their British competitors, to be there, ready and waiting for privatisation.

In France, water is a public issue of political importance. There, the overall responsibility for water lies with the municipalities, and as such it contributes to the power base of local politicians. If, in the great nationalisation wave of 1981–82, the socialists had included the private water companies, they would have earned the wrath of 36,000 mayors all over France[1]—each of whom is well aware that dirty water does not win votes.

In France, water also matters because of that country's humiliating experience during the Occupation (1940–44), when much of her infrastructure was destroyed. It has been said that France's defeat in 1940 was not so much a defeat for the French army as a defeat for French technology. Determined never to give history the opportunity to repeat itself, France has used this defeat positively as a spur to great technological achievements, and, in the period of planning and reconstruction which followed the war,

she set about providing the infrastructure on which economic growth depended, and of which water was a crucial part.[2]

Water also matters in France because of a lack of resources. If rain falls
abundantly on the fertile Paris basin and wheatfields of the north-east, in the
arid south-west of the country water is often in scant supply. Droughts have
worsened in recent years (despite the wash-out of summer 1991). In the
summer of 1989 France's third river, the Garonne, which on its 525 kilometre
journey supplies eleven departments in the south-west with water, dried
up completely.

Table 4.1

The French Water Companies 1988			
National rank	Name	Date founded	Population served
With stakes in British water:			
1.	Compagnie Générale des Eaux and subsidiaries	1853	30 million worldwide, 20 million nationwide
2.	Société Lyonnaise des Eaux and subsidiaries	1880	21 million worldwide, 10 million nationwide
3.	Société d'Aménagement Urbain et Rural (SAUR) and subsidiaries	1933	3.2 million nationwide
In addition:			
4.	Société Eau et Assainissement (SOBEA) and subsidiaries	1878	2.1 million nationwide
5.	Société de Distribution d'Eau Intercommunale (SDEI) and subsidiaries	1929	2 million nationwide
Sources: *Le Livre bleu de l'eau potable; 1988 Annual Reports.*[3]			

But on *this* side of the Channel, water has been taken largely for granted, the
common attitude towards this fundamental but unexciting and alarmingly
invisible industry being summed up by the comment 'flush and forget' (see
above, Chapter 3). Until, that is, French outsiders propelled it to centre stage
by becoming *insiders* in the private water companies, which formed but one
of many planks in their various springboards for European expansion, in
preparation for the watershed of 1992.

So why should three French water companies (see above, Table 4.1) be attracted by a low-key sector of a low-profile industry, of whose existence British investors, at the time when the first Gallic toe tested British water, were scarcely even aware?

Three good reasons for *not* investing in the Statutory Water Companies

Before exploring the reasons why the French chose to invest in the statutory water companies, it is worth remarking that the surprise aroused in British investors when they did was not simply due to the fact that water companies were not regarded as obvious targets for acquisition. There seemed to be sound reasons for not investing in the profit-controlled statutory water companies:

1. their shares earned a very low return on investment;

2. an analysis of the market revealed but limited growth potential.

3. years of capital neglect had meant that huge levels of investment were clearly required to remedy performance shortfalls in order that EC standards might be achieved.[4]

Low return on investment

Prior to the first French acquisition, it had been the case for years that stock in all 28 quoted groups had traded at approximately the same level. The statutory water companies operated under a profits control whereby any surplus above a specified amount had to be refunded to the customer. Dividends were therefore limited to around 3.5 per cent annually. Consequently, those who chose to invest in the private water companies were clearly not getting a large return for their money. One of their few attractions to institutional investors, however, was that water company dividends represented 'franked' income, the advantage of which is that, when paying their own dividends, institutions need make no tax deduction in respect of that proportion of their income gained from investments in the statutory water companies.

Low growth prospects

Demand for water in the UK comes principally from: households; industry; Britain's privately-owned electricity corporations, privatised replacements to the now disbanded Central Electricity Generating Board (CEGB); agriculture and aquiculture (fishfarming and watercress).[5]

Although per capita demand for water in the UK increased at a rate of 3 per cent annually in the three decades of expansion following the war — a period which the French refer to as 'the Thirty Glorious Years', characterised *inter alia* by growing appliance ownership, much of it water-using — the recession which came in the wake of the oil crises of the mid-1970s slowed that growth to an annual average of 0.7 per cent from 1979. It is likely, moreover, that the early 1980s will have seen the start of a saturation in British ownership of certain types of water-using household appliances.[6] So while growth in public demand for water may not yet have levelled out, it is more likely to spring more from population growth on the one hand (forecast at 0.3 per cent per annum), and from the trend towards smaller households on the other, than from increased affluence.[7]

It is anticipated, however, that most of this demand growth will be concentrated in the booming south of England, where the rate of growth of new residential development is fastest, and equally in East Anglia, the country's most rapidly expanding region. In the Wessex area, water put into the public supply has increased by some 16 per cent over the last nine years: at an annual rate of 1.8 per cent, this is more than twice the national average.[8] Moreover, it is in the privileged south that the majority of private water companies are located. Thus, the greater part of the population in the Wessex area (56 per cent) is supplied with water by one of four local water companies.[9]

Meanwhile, direct abstraction by industry has fallen by over 7 per cent annually since 1979. This is due to a combination of factors which include greater efficiency in water use, energy saving investment, the growing tendency for industrial users to receive their water from the public supply, and the sorry decline of Britain's manufacturing base. Likewise, direct abstraction by the CEGB declined by as much as 12 per cent per annum throughout the 1980s, as cooling towers which recycle water replaced power stations which use river water for once-through cooling only. During this time direct abstraction for farm use also decreased at an approximate annual rate of 1.2 per cent. Water use for aquiculture is difficult to measure, since many fish farms are unlicensed.

All in all, for the foreseeable future, demand growth is not expected to exceed an annual average of 1 per cent, almost half of which is likely to be caused by leakages from ageing water mains. So, with the implementation of resource-saving relining and replacement programmes, overall growth may be as low as 0.6 per cent per annum.

The need for high levels of investment

Incentives to invest have been few in the water industry. Traditional British short-termism has been partly responsible, as have public sector spending constraints — in the late 1970s and early 1980s both the private water companies and the water authorities yielded to government pressure to keep price increases below the rate of inflation, effectively precluding much-needed structural repair and investment. And water is also one of the few businesses where capital investment does not boost sales volume.

The environmental improvements exacted by European Commission and customers alike may come at a high marginal cost for marginal change. Pappas, Brigham and Shipley (1983) define a marginal relationship as 'the change in the dependent variable of a function associated with a unitary change in one of the independent variables'.[10] In optimality analysis, the importance of the relationship between marginal and total values lies in the fact that when the marginal is positive the total is increasing, and when the marginal is negative, the total is decreasing, the maximisation of the profit function occurring at that point where the marginal relationship shifts from positive to negative.

The precise cost of purer water is difficult to calculate; but incremental improvements are likely to prove highly expensive. The £3 billion price-tag quoted by the former Environment Secretary Nicholas Ridley in February 1989 as the cost of compliance with EC directives by 1995 very quickly appeared as a gross underestimate.[11] Thereafter, the price was constantly revised upwards, at almost breakneck speed. One month later, the figure of £9 billion was floated by EC officials as the estimated cost of UK compliance with EC standards.[12] The adjustment K factors issued by government to the ten water authorities in July 1989 gave further indication of the huge levels of expenditure required, for they revealed the annual amount by which water services plcs could increase their charges *in real terms* — that is, *above the rate of inflation* — until the year 2000. The average annual increase was to be as much as 5.35 per cent above the Retail Price Index (RPI).[13] By the end of 1989, the government's evaluation of the likely sum involved in implementing water quality standards for drinking water, rivers, bathing water and beaches had escalated to £18.63 billion (Bowers et al., 1989), representing an increase of 700 per cent since the beginning of the year. The capital programme finally agreed with the former regional authorities alone, designed to bring the neglected infrastructure and services up to scratch by the end of the 1990s, carried a price-tag of £26 billion — five times the price at which the industry was sold off in November 1989.[14]

But this is unlikely to be the final bill. By December 1990 a 'small' addendum of £10–15 billion had already been suggested: the estimated cost of full compliance with the NRA's Kinnersley report, which, while the EC's new wastewater directive was being negotiated, proposed rigorous new methods for monitoring the discharges from sewage works. The NRA's discharge proposals, according to one water industry official, would bring into play the law of diminishing returns: 'We would finish up with very high water charges for not very worthwhile improvements. It's all very well championing the environment, but it shouldn't be done regardless of cost'.[15] But even if the recommendations of the Kinnersley report are ignored, compliance with the EC wastewater directive alone — which aims to stop the dumping of sewage sludge at sea by the year 1998 and to enforce higher standards of sewage treatment before its disposal through outfalls — can only be achieved at heavy cost to the industry and its customers.

UBS Phillips and Drew emphasise, moreover, that those aspects of compliance which have been most discussed in the press — the problems of nitrates and pesticides — will not be the largest items on the bill. A 'modest' sum of £1–2 billion, they claim, will cover the cost of the necessary technological development and treatment works.[16] (A Department of Environment report published in 1985 estimated the capital cost of installing denitrifying plants in the UK to be £200 million, and envisaged annual operating expenses at around £20 million — although this does not include compensation for farmers, which would have to be considerable for the programme to be a success.)[17] The *real* drain on the financial resources of the newly privatised plcs anticipated by UBS Phillips and Drew comes rather from the need to rehabilitate mains and service reservoirs, in order that compliance with EC organoleptic parameters (colour, odour, taste) and microbiological parameters (coliforms, faecal streptococci) may be achieved. Total expenditure on mains throughout the 1990s is estimated at some £6–7 billion. An additional £2–3 billion will be required to remedy shortfalls in the performance of sewers. Sewage treatment works also fall short of the mark: as much as 17 per cent of treated sewage in the UK fails to meet the discharge consent conditions laid down by the Control of Pollution Act 1974, Part II (COPA II) (although at Wessex this figure is as low as 6 per cent).[18]

Granted, these figures estimate the cost to the newly privatised water plcs alone, and the private water companies do not deal with sewage. But the most expensive item in the bill — the rehabilitation of water mains — *does* concern them. Given that the water companies had been severely restricted as to the reserves they could accumulate and the amount they could borrow, and given that from the late 1970s onwards successive governments had instructed them to keep their price increases below the prevailing rate of inflation, the need for the rehabilitation of water mains in the areas they serve is unlikely to be less pressing than in the regions served by the newly privatised authorities.

The adjustment K factors for the statutory water companies were not published simultaneously with those of the ten water authorities, despite repeated requests by water company managers that they should be. Instead, the Department of the Environment chose to wait until the water sale had been successfully completed. It must be stressed that 'K', by determining the rate and frequency of price increases, sets the balance sheet for years to come. But when the K factors for the private water companies were finally released in 1990, they were found to be *considerably lower* than those issued to the water authorities some months previously; the water companies had not therefore been granted the 'level playing-field' they had so desperately sought.[19]

Three good reasons for investing in the Statutory Water Companies

If the private water companies really are the 'lame ducks' which the above analysis might seem to suggest, why then were the French so interested in them? And interested they were: the extent of their interest may be gauged by the amount each invested in Britain's statutory water companies in the short space of a year: between £97 and £144 million per company on outright bids alone. Or it may be measured by an examination of water company ownership twelve months after the first French acquisition (see below, Table 4.2), by which time Biwater, a private UK contractor, and Southern Water Authority had also joined the fray.

By 1989, Générale des Eaux, Lyonnaise des Eaux and SAUR had shares in the water market of England and Wales of approximately 4.8 per cent, 5.2 per cent and 3.1 per cent respectively. This compared with market share in their own backyard of 54 per cent for Générale des Eaux, 27 per cent for Lyonnaise des Eaux, 8.5 per cent for SAUR (and 5 per cent each for SOGEA and SDEI) (Malandain and Tavernier, 1991).

Table 4.2

Ownership of Britain's Statutory Water Companies 1989 (as percentage of voting capital)				
	SWC	RWA Area	Stake[†]	Bid
General Utilities	Tendring Hundred	Anglian	100.0	10.0m
(CGE subsidiary)	South Staffordshire	Severn Trent	26.1	
	Folkestone	Southern	100.0	11.5m
	Mid Kent	Southern	100.0	30.0m
	Colne Valley	Thames	28.2	
	Lee Valley	Thames	100.0	41.0m
	North Surrey	Thames	100.0	15.6m
	Rickmansworth	Thames	16.1	
	Bristol	Wessex	29.9	
TOTAL				108.1m
Lyonnaise UK	East Anglian	Anglian	100.0	21.6m
	Essex	Anglian	100.0	47.6m
	Newcastle & G'head	Northumbrian	100.0	39.1m
	Sunderland	Northumbrian	100.0	35.9m
	Bristol	Wessex	18.0	
TOTAL				144.2m

Table 4.2 (cont.)

Ownership of Britain's Statutory Water Companies 1989 (as percentage of voting capital)				
SAUR	Eastbourne	Southern	100.0	15.0m
Water Services	Mid Kent	Southern	16.6	
	Mid Sussex	Southern	100.0	16.8m
	West Kent	Southern	100.0	7.4m
	Colne Valley	Thames	25.0	
	Mid Southern	Thames	100.0	58.6m
	Rickmansworth	Thames	27.7	
	Wrexham	Welsh	11.0	
TOTAL				97.8m
Biwater	East Worcestershire	Severn Trent	100.0	2.98m
	Bournemouth	Wessex	100.0	17.6m
	West Hampshire	Wessex	100.0	10.0m
TOTAL				30.6m
Southern	Eastbourne	Southern	25.0	
	Folkestone	Southern	25.0	
	Mid Sussex	Southern	25.0	
	West Kent	Southern	25.0	
AIPF‡	Mid Kent	Southern	1.8	
	East Surrey	Thames	28.0	
	Sutton	Thames	13.7	

Sources: Articles appearing in the *Financial Times*,[20] and UBS Phillips
and Drew report, *The Water Industry in England and Wales*.
† Where a company has full control (i.e. equal or greater than 30 per
cent) 100 per cent holding is given.
‡ Associated Insurance Pension Fund, a private investment vehicle for
Mr Duncan Saville, a Sydney-based businessman.

Their reasons for buying into the British market were the following:

1. With little market share left to bite at in France, they sought *expansion* into other water markets abroad.

2. They aimed to use their acquisitions as a platform for *diversification* into local authority contracting by fostering local links and exploiting their customer base.

3. The purchase of statutory water companies carries with it the possibility of accessing valuable *land assets*, whereas in France, where the functions of ownership and management are fully divorced, the French water companies are the operators of assets which belong to the local municipalities. This land might subsequently be used for lucrative commercial purposes.

Expansion into other water industry markets

Olivier Celier, international development manager at SAUR, compares the expansionist drive of the French water companies to that of five rats in a cage, desperate for escape.[21] The possibilities for expansion at home were limited. The French water industry is 85 per cent wrapped up in contracts which often stretch for thirty years. Share movement at the Paris Bourse, moreover, is impeded by crossed shareholdings (where corporate allies hold major stakes in one another), *autocontrôle* (where a company's shares are safely held by its own subsidiaries),[22] secret shareholder pacts and the existence of corporate structures which radically reduce shareholders' powers (Hamdouch, 1989). The elected strategy of each of the big trio was therefore to consolidate its position in France, and pursue growth elsewhere.

In the early 1980s, the French water companies ventured abroad, winning contracts to supply water in developing countries. Then, in the late 1980s, they recognised the enormous potential of the UK, incisively and ingeniously penetrating the market by a route which others had overlooked. Their respective turnovers are a good measure of the empires they have built. In 1979, for example, Générale des Eaux had a turnover of FF 8 billion, about £0.8 billion. By 1988, sales had soared to FF 85.2 billion — a tenfold increase in almost as many years.[23] As the general manager of one independent British water company observed, on hearing that a subsidiary of Générale des Eaux, Société Générale d'Entreprise, had purchased a controlling stake in the British civil engineering company Norwest Holst, 'How many other organisations are being whittled down? When Britain wakes up, it will be too late. There will be a closed shop'.[24]

But these empires are probably but pale shadows of what they may one day become. Lyonnaise des Eaux invested in the UK water market as part of what chairman Jérôme Monod terms his group's 'European growth strategy'.[25] The group's objective is to gain significant market share in *all* of its businesses in *all* of the countries of the single market. By 'significant market share', Monod understands between 5 and 25 per cent of each national market. This he aims to achieve through a combination of acquisitions, as in the UK, and alliances; for time is too short for home-grown expansion. By the late 1980s, Monod saw his group as having a sound European base which was becoming ever stronger; his aspiration, however, was for a global presence. In July 1990, a merger between Lyonnaise des Eaux and the French construction group Dumez — a company with global market share which nevertheless sought to reposition itself for 1992 — was concluded.[26] The merger, which Monod described as the 'alliance of water and concrete', gave rise to a formidable group with an annual turnover of FF 82 billion.[27]

The French have clearly grasped the importance of gaining market share. Indeed, the quest for market share has become one of the dominant strands in French business strategy in the 1990s. When competition is at its fiercest —and with 1992 in the offing, the heat is on—having market share is the key to profitability (Kerin and Peterson, 1983).[28] And although *gaining* market share can be a major drain on resources (both Générale des Eaux and Lyonnaise des Eaux made additional share issues in March 1989, raising FF 3.3 billion and FF 2.7 billion respectively), the French water suppliers have clearly taken a conscious decision to withstand higher costs in the short run in order to strengthen the market position of each of their businesses in the long run. By 1992, the European market may indeed be largely wrapped up.

Diversification into local authority contracting

For the French companies do not intend to expand in water services alone. Their empires have been built on a formula of expansion in the core business and diversification into related areas. Générale des Eaux's water distribution and waterworks construction division accounts for no more than 22.2 per cent of the group's consolidated global sales. Other divisions include public works and building construction (contributing 37.7 per cent of turnover); energy management (10.6 per cent); electrical contracting and power generation (7.9 per cent); urban maintenance, embracing healthcare, leisure and recreational activities, cable television, municipal transport, building maintenance and management, parks and gardens maintenance and car park management (4.7 per cent); real estate development (4.4 per cent); fuel trading (3.7 per cent); and home building (1.4 per cent), with additional services and contracting accounting for the remainder (7.4 per cent).[29]

Related diversification proved possible because of the privileged relationship which the French water suppliers were able to develop with the local municipalities over a period of many years. Since local customers came to regard the water companies as fundamentally reliable, here was a chance to use that well-disposed customer base to launch a whole host of other related and unrelated services, such as refuse collection, waste disposal, heating (from the incineration of household waste) for sheltered housing, sheltered housing itself, other forms of property development, healthcare, funeral services, even cable television, mobile phones, golf and theme parks.

The conjuncture in the UK in the late 1980s could not therefore have been more welcoming to the French, with the privatisation of the water industry coinciding with the deregulation of local authority service contracting. Ownership of existing water companies with a good local reputation has enabled the French suppliers to surmount the hurdle of getting on the tender list. Already, Egham-based Sitaclean Technology, owned by Lyonnaise des Eaux, has won several local government contracts for waste collection;[30] as indeed has Cory Onyx (better known simply as Onyx), a joint venture created in November 1988 by Compagnie Générale d'Entreprise, a subsidiary of Générale des Eaux specialising in municipal waste collection, and Cory Waste Management, part of the British-owned Ocean Transport and Trading group. More ambitiously, Associated Heat Services (AHS), a British-based subsidiary of Générale des Eaux headed by Lord Ezra, the former chairman of British Coal, is currently seeking the contract to sell cheap electricity from France, imported through a 2,000-megawatt cable link beneath the Channel. This will enable AHS to undercut the price of British-produced electricity following the privatisation of the industry in the autumn of 1990 and the spring of 1991.[31] In April 1991, the European Commission announced that existing barriers to cross-border sales of electricity within the Community, which hitherto had accounted for a fraction of electricity sold within the Community, a mere 3 per cent, were to be removed. France, which already exports some 8 per cent of national electricity output, produced at over thirty pressurised water reactor nuclear power stations (Barsoux and Lawrence, 1990), is well placed to take advantage of this. And Associated Gas Services, a subsidiary of AHS established in 1989, is already challenging British Gas (and Quadrant, a joint venture formed by Esso and Shell), vying with the privatised giant for the contract to supply the Midland Gas Consortium, a group of local authorities based in the Midlands (Chapman, 1990). As one water chief pertinently remarked, 'This is a bear hug; and it has claws'.[32]

It is worth noting that even before the water sale was complete, the ten newly privatised water authorities had already begun to emulate the French by investigating proposals to diversify into related — and unrelated — activities. These included overseas consultancy, plumbing, engineering and contracting services, construction, waste management, and in one particular case, cable television.[33]

When, in August 1989, Northumbrian Water, the smallest of the water authorities, announced its decision to diversify into cable television through a joint venture with Starstream, a small US cable company, it was the first of the ten to embark on a venture outside its core business. Northumbrian would do well to pay heed to the findings of a recent study on diversification by l'Ecole des Mines (one of the exclusive group of French *Grandes Ecoles*, France's elite engineering and management schools), which warns that only those companies which have a clear idea of their own skills and strengths are likely to succeed with moves into unrelated areas.[34] As a newcomer to the private sector, Northumbrian is also a novice to open competition, and as such should be wary of attempting to run before it can walk; it has taken the French suppliers almost 150 years to get to where they are now. Successful diversification depends, after all, on *synergies* (Johnson and Scholes, 1988). And since synergies are 'concerned with the desired characteristics of fit between the firm and its new product-market entries'

(Ansoff, 1965),[35] it is clear that synergies are more likely to result from moves into *related* activities. In the expanding market of household waste incineration, for instance, Générale des Eaux is able to capitalise on the increasing synergies arising between the fields of energy and waste management, two of the group's core businesses. As Joseph T. Wright warned, 'While diversification is fine as a matter of abstract principle, it can result in so many different eggs in one basket that nothing really significant is hatched out of them'.[36] The message to Northumbrian would seem to be this: when in doubt, 'stick to your knitting!' (Peters and Waterman, 1982). Or, as one financial journalist put it, 'Make it lean, mean and centred on a core business'.[37]

The possibility of accessing valuable land assets

The third and final reason why the French have sought to penetrate the British water market is that this carries with it the possibility of accessing valuable land assets. For Britain's private water companies and newly privatised authorities are all major landowners. In all, they 'own' a grand total of 455,765 acres.

This matter of 'ownership', however, requires some elucidation. The Water Act of 1973 transferred ownership of land assets, water and sewerage systems from local authorities to the then newly-created public water authorities, without any compensation being paid. It is therefore questionable whether the water plcs have any right to this land at all. Fifteen local councils in such cities as Birmingham, Manchester, Liverpool, Sheffield, Hull and Exeter are seeking to claim compensation retrospectively. As Chapman writes in *Selling the Family Silver*:

> [A new set of politicians] decided they should hand back to us the businesses we already supposed to own. But instead of giving them back to us, they made us pay for them. This meant spending tens of millions of pounds in fees on intermediaries in the City of London, which helped them through a sticky patch but cost us dear. When we had spent our savings to buy these businesses back from ourselves, the Government then decided to give us some of this money back through tax cuts, so that we would re-elect them to carry out more of the same. If there is a winner in all this, it is not the public.[38]

To three companies which had never been able to own their asset base in France, the possibility of accessing valuable land assets proved to be an alluring proposition. Strict government safeguards are to be implemented to ensure both that 'countryside areas of special conservation and amenity value' are protected from development abuse, and that surplus land assets are used for the benefit of customers.[39] But for any company wishing to develop its land for whatever commercial purpose, there is a simple loophole: it need only transfer ownership to a subsidiary to avoid government controls.[40] It is the opinion of this writer that the loophole is deliberate. The management teams of Britain's water plcs are to be confined to regulatory strait-jackets in their core business, and as a result, they may be forced to make their profits elsewhere. Were non-core activities also to be subject to regulatory scrutiny, were the water plcs to be constantly looking over their shoulder here too, there would be a real danger that every last vestige of entrepreneurship would be stifled out of them (see below, Chapter 7). Fearing a proliferation of subsidiaries charged with maximising returns on land holdings, environmental economists warn of the construction interests of the three French water companies (Bowers et al., 1988). As we noted above, the most lucrative of Générale des Eaux's divisions is its building division. Lyonnaise des Eaux has merged with a powerful construction group. And SAUR is the subsidiary of one of the largest construction companies in the world, the mighty Bouygues. As water companies, they will be in a privileged position to facilitate or impede the development schemes of their competitors in the construction industry because of the importance of their providing — or refusing to provide — water and sewerage infrastructure.

The grounds for caution: why the French should tread warily

The French should not be overly concerned by the low growth prospects of the water market outlined above. As the discussion of the diversification plans of both French and British water companies has illustrated, the future development of the water industry is not rooted in core operations alone, and in the 1990s, we can expect to see the newly privatised water plcs branching out into other related areas. Nor should the French companies be deterred by capital expenditure uncertainties: the loophole of 'cost pass-through' is likely to ensure that customers will bear the brunt of new financial burdens on the industry.

But the future is not all rosy. There are serious grounds for caution, and these concern the value of statutory water company shares:

1. In the run-up to privatisation, at the time when the K factors for the 28 private water companies were being negotiated, water company managers laid much stress on the need for a return on capital which would be comparable to that of the water services plcs. They sought, in other words, a 'level playing-field'. There can be little doubt that this has been denied them. Concerned that there should be no increase in water charges which would be directly attributable to water privatisation itself, the Department of the Environment was determined to keep water company K figures as low as possible. That the DoE did not publish these simultaneously with those of the ten water authorities, as water company managers had requested, and further, that it

waited until the water sale was successfully completed to do so, should
have served as a warning.

When the K figures were finally released in 1990, they were found
to be lower that those allocated to the water services plcs. Granted,
there was considerable variation between individual water suppliers,
but the general trend was low, with minus figures creeping in after a
few years for several companies (Cambridge, East Worcestershire and
West Kent), whereas none had been issued to privatised authorities.

Differentiation on the part of the DoE in favour of the water authorities is further exemplified by its treatment of a proposed joint venture
(to build a reservoir) by Southern Water plc, and Mid Kent and Folkestone water companies. In financial terms, Mid Kent were the senior
partners in the venture, the company's need for the reservoir (at Broad
Oak) being greater than that of the former authority. Southern's estimated share of the cost, however, was taken into account in the setting
of its K figure, yet Mid Kent's share of the burden was to be left to
'cost pass-through'. This can only result in substantial increases in
charges to the company's customers when construction begins in 1994,
while their neighbours in Southern's area of supply will continue to be
charged according to the agreed K formula.

Lame ducks the private water companies are not, but their low K figures seem to be designed to leave them as sitting ducks for takeover
— if not by neighbouring water services plcs, given Ofwat's anxiety to
preserve the maximum number of comparators in the industry, then
perhaps by other predators: companies engaged in the supply of pipes
or pumps, for example, or the construction and design of treatment
plants such as Biwater. Given the low K figures assigned to the private water companies, it is difficult to see how their share values can
be maintained; shares in Britain's statutory water companies may soon
be worth but a fraction of the amount paid for them by the French
water suppliers.

2. The ability of shareholders to access land value will be crucial in sup-
    porting statutory water company share prices at their current levels. In
    the opinion of UBS Phillips and Drew, however, this access is unlikely
    to be forthcoming. This will leave only Southern Water and possibly
    the construction company Biwater with sound reasons for purchasing
    the shares (scale effects and vertical integration respectively).[41]

The grounds for caution: why the British should tread warily

The way was cleared for Britain's ten water services plcs to invest in the
private water sector when both the High Court and former Secretary of
State for the Environment, Nicholas Ridley, gave their blessing.[42] Yet the

way ahead is unlikely to be one of plain sailing:

1.   After privatisation, some shake-up in the French position was almost
     inevitable. Would we witness, as some had warned that we would,
     the *dénouement* of a French conspiracy? — a carve-up of Britain's water
     companies, a *fait accompli*?
         If the charge of formal, explicit collusion was angrily denied by the
     trio, that of informal, tacit collusion was less easy to disclaim. To
     Générale des Eaux, the north and west of London; to Lyonnaise des
     Eaux, the eastern seaboard; to SAUR, a large chunk of the Southern
     region. If only because of the paucity of sellers, none of the three is free
     to act independently of the others (Scherer, 1980).[43] Oligopoly therefore
     exists, and 'collusion' — if only that form of collusion which comes from
     years of cohabitation, and from knowing each others' businesses like
     one's own — might not be far behind.
         In September 1990 it emerged that Lyonnaise des Eaux and Générale
     des Eaux *were* willing to work together *abroad*, although not on
     home territory. In an article in *L'Expansion* entitled 'Lyonnaise des
     Eaux-Dumez makes overtures to Générale', Managing Director Jérôme
     Monod announced, 'There is much we can do together with Générale
     des Eaux, particularly in foreign countries in need of international aid,
     in the East or Vietnam for instance. I am personally in favour of it.' Al-
     ready, it transpired, the two rivals had embarked on a joint wastewater
     project in Kuala Lumpur.[44]

2.   Nevertheless, however opposed the water plcs are to French ownership
     of British water, they should bear in mind two important points.
         First, alliances — which the French companies are actively seeking
     with newly privatised authorities — are preferable to acquisitions. Part-
     nerships are reciprocal arrangements where two parties collaborate for
     mutual benefit from a position of comparative equality, and jointly reap
     the fruits of their efforts (Sharp and Shearman, 1987); but takeover im-
     plies the surrender of overall control. There are many areas in which
     collaboration might prove possible, and research and development —
     in order that a larger combined sum of money might be better spent on
     improving the quality of our water, without the repetition of projects
     on both sides of the Channel — is a particularly obvious one. Collabo-
     ration between European firms can help to foster a win-win situation
     in Europe. Antagonism towards European competitors will ensure that
     we never get beyond a win-lose situation. Few of the newly privatised
     authorities, however, are interested in talking to the French, perhaps
     because, after the French infiltration of the private water companies,
     they cannot but regard them as threatening.
         Second, there is one aspect of the marketing of water shares abroad
     which is worthy of comment. Although shares were marketed in Eu-

rope, Canada and the United States, it was *in Japan* that the overseas privatisation campaign was at its peak. Only there was information placed in newspapers and sent directly to private investors.[45] And Japanese investors were accorded 7.3 per cent of the share issue, as against only 3.6 per cent for the whole of continental Europe.[46] No doubt this was essentially a marketing decision, rather than a political one: after all, there had been a good Japanese take-up of previous privatisation issues. Nevertheless, it seems to this particular writer that greater overtures to Europe—and perhaps in particular to the French, who had shown their commitment to the British market by setting up subsidiaries here—might have made more sense. As Chapman argues, 'Since Britain is part of the European Community—and since it is only a matter of time before there is political and economic union—it also makes sense to open up all privatizations to Europeans'.[47] One thing is undeniable: Japanese investors, from the other side of the globe, have far less reason to care about the quality of British water than our near neighbours in the European Community.

Summary of conclusions

There were good reasons for not investing in the British water market in 1987–88: shares in Britain's statutory water companies had consistently earned a low return, the market seemed to hold but limited growth potential, and there was an urgent need of capital expenditure. However, the French had powerful motives of their own for investing in British water. First, with limited possibilities for expansion in France, it made sense to turn abroad. Second, they aimed to use their purchases as a platform for diversification into local authority contracting. Third, they were enticed by valuable land assets, which they lacked at home. Their overriding motivation was to gain as much market share for each of their businesses as possible.

Yet the picture is not all rosy, and grounds for caution remain. It is conceivable, for instance, that the value of statutory water company shares may plummet in response to lower-than-expected adjustment K factors on the one hand, and the failure of shareholders to access land value on the other. Meanwhile, British water companies might find themselves confounded by inter-firm collaboration on the part of the French investors in Britain as well as further afield. Nevertheless, it is the opinion of this writer that Franco-British collaboration, particularly in the sphere of research and development projects, makes a good deal of sense, while selling water shares to Japan may well turn out to be 'money down the drain'.

Notes

1. Personal interview, July 1989.

2. See Landes, D. S. (1969), *The Unbound Prometheus: technological change in Western Europe from 1750 to the present*, Cambridge University Press, Cambridge, pp. 496–7.

3. Population served by SOBEA and SDEI refer to the year 1979, as given in *Le Livre bleu de l'eau potable*, op. cit, p. 44.

4. The blame for this lack of capital investment ought not to be laid at the door of the private water companies. Limited as to the reserves they could accumulate and the amount they could borrow, they had been bound hand and foot by a succession of short-sighted governments. In particular, recent Conservative governments had told them to keep their price increases lower than the prevailing rate of inflation, thus reducing their ability to invest even further.

5. See UBS Phillips and Drew, op. cit., pp. 16–18.

6. Approximate ownership of key water-using appliances in the UK in the early 1980s was as follows: WC–99 per cent; Bath–95 per cent; Shower–25 per cent; Washing Machine–75 per cent; Dishwasher–3 per cent. Reported in UBS Phillips and Drew, op. cit., p. 17.

7. The average size of British households is expected to decline throughout the remainder of this century. Thus, married couples are predicted to decrease in number from 10,835,000 in 1981 to 10,746,000 twenty years later. Consequently, lone-parent and one-person households are expected to increase from 1,373,000 and 3,919,000 in 1981 to 1,832,000 and 5,653,000 respectively by the year 2001. Source: Department of the Environment, 1986.

8. Cited in the *Water Share Offers mini prospectus*, issued 29 November 1989, p. 24.

9. ibid.

10. Pappas, J. L., Brigham, E. F. and Shipley, B., op. cit., p. 39.

11. See 'Water users face £3bn bill if EC standards are met', *Financial Times*, 23 February 1989, p. 1.

12. See 'EC standards "may cost £9bn"', op. cit.

13. The K factors for the ten water authorities, as announced in August 1989, are as follows: Anglian: 5.5 per cent; Northumbrian: 7 per cent;† North West: 5 per cent; Severn Trent: 5.5 per cent;‖ Southern: 5.5 per cent;‡ South West: 6.5 per cent;† Thames: 4.5 per cent; Welsh: 6.5 per cent;† Wessex: 4.5 per cent; and Yorkshire: 3 per cent. Listed in the *Water Share Offers mini prospectus*, op. cit.
    † The K factors of authorities marked thus are to be reduced after five years.
    ‡ Southern's K is 5.5 per cent for three years, 3.5 per cent for two years, 0 per cent thereafter.

14. Quoted in 'Swift currents below the surface', op. cit.

15. ibid.

16. UBS Phillips and Drew, op. cit., p. 20.

17. See 'Counting the cost of purer water', *Financial Times*, 28 November 1989, p. 40.

18. Two types of consents are allowed: descriptive consents apply to works serving a population of less than 250; numeric consents, stating effluent discharge quality, apply to the vast majority. The main effect of COPA II was to allow public access to information on discharge, and to permit prosecution by private individuals should authorities be in breach of consent. The EC directives governing sewage are those which concern the quality of bathing water (76/160/EEC) and the correct disposal of sewage sludge on land (86/278/EEC). A further directive on waste water treatment is currently under consideration. If agreed, water companies operating in coastal regions would have to stop dumping untreated waste at sea.

19. The K figure for the private water companies are given in *Water Supply Companies Factbook* (1990), published by the Water Companies' Association.

20. See in particular 'Water companies appeal on stock build-up', *Financial Times*, 23 December 1988, p. 8, 'Water industry defies efforts to control its flow', *Financial Times*, 12 January 1989, p. 8, and 'A long view from across the Channel', *Financial Times*, Survey on 'the Water Industry', 25 July 1989, p. 14.

21. See 'Riding the crest of a corporate wave', *Financial Times*, 22 April 1989, p. 11.

22. In 1989 the French Senate voted to abolish *autocontrôle* by July 1991, but it is clear that such crossed shareholdings will prove extremely tricky to undo.

23. Cited in the Compagnie Générale des Eaux Annual Report for 1988, p. 7.

24. Personal interview with the author, June 1989. See also 'French group aiming to take controlling stake in Norwest', *Financial Times*, 17 January 1989, p. 22.

25. Quoted in 'Why a French supplier is bubbling with enthusiasm for British water', op. cit.

26. See the illuminating article by Bournois, F. and Chauchat, J.-H. (1990), 'Managing managers in Europe, *European Journal of Management*, vol. 8, no. 1, p. 11.

27. Cited in 'Le groupe Lyonnaise des eaux-Dumez représente un chiffre d'affaires de 82 milliards de francs', *Le Monde*, 11 July 1990.

28. Kerin, R. A. and Peterson, R. A. (1983), *Perspectives in Strategic Marketing Management*, Allyn and Bacon, Boston, p. 237.

29. These percentages refer to the year 1988. See CGE Annual Report for 1988, op. cit., p. 15.

30. See for example 'French switch attention from water to waste collection', *Financial Times*, 28 April 1989, p. 10.

31. 'Company seeks cheap French power deal', *Financial Times*, 14 September 1989, p. 10.

32. Personal interview with the author, June 1989.

33. See 'Water authority plans to diversify into cable TV', *Financial Times*, 18 August 1989, p. 8.

34. The findings of this survey are published in 'The ups and downs of diversifying away from the core', *Financial Times*, 11 August 1989, p. 11.

35. Cited in Ansoff, op. cit., p. 79.

36. ibid, p. 117.

37. See 'More baskets, choicier eggs', *The Economist*, 21 October 1989, p. 107.

38. From Chapman, C., op. cit., pp. ix – x.

39. See 'Water chiefs aim to save land sale profits for investors', *Independent*, 21 February 1989, p. 8.

40. 'Water companies face curb on selling land of "special value"', *Financial Times*, 3 May 1989, p. 14.

41. UBS Phillips and Drew, op. cit., p. 46.

42. See, for example, 'Court clears way for UK water takeovers', *Financial Times*, 22 December 1988, p. 1.

43. Scherer, F. M. (1980), *Industrial Market Structure and Economic Performance*, 2nd edition, Rand McNally, London, pp. 199-227.

44. Cited in 'La Lyonnaise des Eaux-Dumez tend la main à la Générale', *L'Expansion*, September 1990, p. 38.

45. Institutional investors in Canada and the US were awarded 1.6 per cent and 1.3 per cent of the share issue respectively. See 'Buoyant debut for water likely as institutions chase shares', *Financial Times*, 12 December 1989, p. 1.

46. See, for example, 'Water to Japan', *Financial Times*, 23 May 1989, p. 20.

47. Chapman, C., op. cit., p. 193.

5 The French Agents for Change: opportunity or threat ? — a balance sheet

There is nothing more difficult to take in hand, more perilous to conduct,
or more uncertain of success than to take a lead in the introduction of
a new order of things, because the innovation has for enemies all those
who have done well under the old conditions and lukewarm defenders in
those who may do well under the new — (Machiavelli).

The triggers which brought about radical change in the British water industry in the late 1980s were multiple: the trend towards denationalisation; the move towards accountability in public services; the efficiency drive which accompanied the removal of state subsidies; a heightened environmental awareness on the part of the public at large; much publicised incidents of water pollution; and the arrival of three diversified, cash-rich French water suppliers, who, in the quest for market share in Europe and in the short space of a year, sent the value of water company stock rocketing.[1] The combined effect of these change agents was to turn ten administrative bodies, with little sense of either image or identity, into water businesses which sought to manage themselves, to expand and diversify into other areas, and which were self-aware and market-conscious in a way in which they had never been before.

Change is usually a necessary response to the presence of opportunity or threat in the competitive environment. But however necessary, it is often an unwelcome visitor.[2] The well-known maxim 'no gain without pain' springs to mind. Administrators, according to Ian MacGregor (1987), seek to preserve the status quo. The reverse side of the coin is the potentiality which change carries with it: it is the essence of management to identify the need for change and to have the will to effect it, to strive for efficiency and improvement (see above, Chapter 3).

The nature of opportunity or threat, however, can be complex. In the first place, they are rarely mutually exclusive. This chapter therefore seeks to be alive to the threat in opportunity and the opportunity in threat. Competitive rivalry, moreover, can spring from some unlikely sources. Porter

observes that 'competition in an industry is rooted in its underlying economics, and competitive forces exist that go well beyond the established
combatants in a particular industry'.[3] Johnson and Scholes (1988) isolate
four key forces for consideration: the threat of substitutes; the power of
suppliers; the power of buyers; and the threat of entry. Water, however, is
without substitute. The British water companies, moreover, are their own
suppliers. Buyer power is weak, since there is no alternative source of supply (each firm operates an effective monopoly in its own area), and since the
volume of their purchases tends to be low. So the competitive force which
is of greatest importance to the British water suppliers has to do with the
threat of entry, particularly since government action, in the form of privatisation, has dismantled the critical entry barrier. Meanwhile the other
key barrier to entry, the enormous capital outlay required, has proved ineffectual against the French giants, whose shareholders are wealthy French
companies.[4] The present chapter therefore seeks to weigh up, in the cold
light of day, the benefits and drawbacks of the French involvement to the
principle stakeholders concerned:

1   the newly privatised water authorities;
2   the statutory water companies
3   shareholders of the above;
4   customers of the above;
5   unions and employees;
6   the environment.

Differences between the above perspectives will be highlighted, and an
explanation sought.

The impact of the French involvement on the water plcs

To a large extent, the newly privatised water authorities were not as directly
affected by the French penetration of the market as the private water companies. After all, they had not been targets for acquisition — first because
they were publicly owned; then because of their size; and next because of
the government's 'golden share' provision, limiting foreign holdings in the
water plcs to 15 per cent for five years from flotation (possibly for ten), and
thereby warding off unwelcome post-privatisation takeover by a foreign
group.[5]

   Yet the water plcs *are* directly concerned by the 'Trojan horse' which the
three French distributors have succeeded in constructing in their own backyard. Where one of the trio owns several private water companies in any
one region, their amalgamation would create a substantial competitor for
the water plc of that area. Since January 1989, however, bids for one or more
water companies with combined assets in excess of £30 million are automat-

ically referred to the Monopolies and Mergers Commission. Moreover, the Water Act of 1989 has ruled that the number of independently controlled comparator companies can only be reduced given significant benefits to the public.

These restrictions were put to the test by the proposed merger of Lee Valley, Colne Valley and Rickmansworth water companies in the densely-populated, rapidly-expanding South East, first mooted in the summer of 1989.[6] 'Three Valleys Water Services', as the new company intended to call itself, would have a market capitalisation of some £100 million and a customer base of 2.3 million in London and the Home Counties. The value of its land-bank alone would be enormous, assuming that this could be accessed (see above, Chapter 4).[7] And, what is more, its largest shareholder would be Générale des Eaux.[8]

The MMC pondered long and hard over its decision, which was not announced until April 1990, by which time the water sell-off had been safely completed and the market début of the new water plcs successfully accomplished. In the event, the MMC reached the conclusion that any detrimental effects which a reduction in the number of independent companies would cause might be offset by estimated cost savings of £60 million, which could then be passed on to the customer.[9] Yet the merger was not at this stage allowed to proceed. Nicholas Ridley, who became Trade and Industry Secretary after his spell at the DoE, blocked the deal because he was not convinced that such cost savings would be sufficient to outweigh the disadvantage of a reduction in the number of operators, upon which the government's concept of 'comparative competition' depended. One can imagine, too, that neighbouring Thames Water may have used its considerable lobbying skills to impede the creation of what would be the UK's seventh largest water supplier on its very doorstep.

The City, excited by the prospect of a wave of mergers in the newly privatised industry, reacted badly to the news, and water shares slumped. But the DTI's decision was not final. A further investigation by the Director General of Water Services ordered by Nicholas Ridley identified greater savings than had previously been anticipated, and in August 1990, after more than a year of deliberation, the planned merger was at last able to proceed.

The close proximity of substantial French competitors may well disrupt water plc plans; but it thereby forces a strategy overhaul on to their agenda. For competition, as one of Générale des Eaux's top managers insists, is often a 'spur to better performance'.[10] There is now a growing understanding, moreover, that strategy and culture are closely related, and that culture must sometimes be moulded for strategy to succeed. Miles and Snow (1978) describe organisations as either 'defenders' or 'prospectors'. While the former are organisations whose prevailing beliefs are fundamentally conservative, and where low-risk strategies, secure markets and well-tried potential solutions are valued, the latter are organisations whose dominant beliefs have to do with innovation and breaking new ground.[11] As a spur to better performance, the French are helping the water plcs to take a crucial step out of their predominantly 'defender' culture in the direction of the 'prospectors'. Competition from them at home and abroad will help to sharpen the strategic focus which the water plcs need to compete: there never was competitive advantage without competition (Ohmae, 1987).[12] Likewise, without a particular goal or destination in mind, any direction, it is said, will get you there. If, in 1979, the water industry was one of several state-owned industries to lack a published financial target, in 1989 the French offered an example of what might be achieved. And as fully diversified companies with interests ranging from golf to cable television, theme parks to mobile phones, the French were clearly helping the water plcs out of the rut of being viewed as dull by the market. (The ensuing recession helped too: in 1990, perceived as a safe bet in bad times, water shares proved to be the stock markets's best performing sector).[13]

Of course, the water plcs must not embrace high-risk strategies too hastily. However great their desire for expansion, the need to invest, to lay firm foundations, is more pressing. Nevertheless, the element of adventure which the French have introduced into a formerly stagnant industry is much welcomed by water chiefs, several of whom had enjoyed far more exciting careers in business prior to their entry into Britain's low-profile, somnolent water industry. Roy Watts of Thames Water, for instance, had enjoyed a highly successful career at British Airways, and had been tipped by many as the man most likely to lead the company into the private sector as its chief executive; although in the event Colin Marshall of Avis was given the top job.[14] So for some, life has been more stimulating since the French involvement. As one water authority chairman put it: 'The French have added some spice to life, and we thank them for it'.[15]

The water plcs might also benefit from the French involvement by actively seeking ways in which French and British water suppliers can work together as partners, in the UK or elsewhere. While Japan and the US operate as nation states, Europe remains a plurality. However, as Ohmae points out, in a complex, uncertain world filled with dangerous opponents — a world of converging consumer tastes, rapidly spreading and 'turbulent' technology, and escalating fixed costs — it makes sense not to go it alone.[16] There is a growing belief that the future of Europe will be dominated by alliances and networks between different international groups. The corporate image which Lyonnaise des Eaux seeks to project is precisely that of a 'global network of mutually supportive companies'.[17] Similarly, both Générale des Eaux and SAUR describe themselves not as multinationals but rather as 'conglomerates of local businesses'.[18] In the late 1980s, the forging of alliances was high on French business agenda. One, in April 1990, between the French public-sector flagship, Renault, and the privately-owned Swedish car manufacturer Volvo, broke the mould of the French state-owned company: it was a public acknowledgement of the fact that, with the opening up of markets, state ownership was no longer deemed sufficient to guarantee survival and prosperity, even in better times. So, Ohmae insists, 'Globalisation mandates alliances and makes them absolutely essential to strategy'.[19] But these networks and alliances are being formed *now*. Those who choose to wait may well find themselves frozen out later on.

It seems then that the government's 'golden share' ruling may have given the water plcs a chance which was perhaps unintentional: the 15 per cent ceiling on foreign holdings has left them free to form partnerships *of their own choosing*. The ball is in their court. Collaboration with other European groups offers a number of advantages, providing a modicum of protection while simultaneously confronting Britain's privatised authorities with more competition than hitherto, as the national market is opened up to European and international competition: 'In this sense [collaboration] may be a useful way of weaning firms used to privileged access to national markets and forcing them to face the realities of global competition' (Sharp and Shearman, 1987).[20] Teaming-up also facilitates pre-competitive research and product development, which, with ever shortening product life cycles and the ever more exacting environmental standards demanded by Brussels, may prove prohibitively expensive to firms which choose to work alone.

Whether or not the water plcs now seize that opportunity still remains to be seen. Expressing his keenness to collaborate with water authorities, public or private, the chairman of Lyonnaise des Eaux, Jérôme Monod, commented that he preferred partnerships to acquisitions, which quickly exhaust financial resources.[21] One water authority chairman interviewed by the author admitted that his water authority was 'talking to the French'.[22] His employees have also undergone intensive training in several European languages with a language consultancy consortium, a member of the national Language-Export-Centre network. For firms which aspire to be nothing more than targets for takeover, language is not a problem; for those proactive firms which seek to retain control, perhaps through forming wider alliances beyond national boundaries, the language problem must be addressed.[23]

But Monod doubts whether partnerships with the privatised water authorities will now prove to be forthcoming. His pessimism is shared by Jean-Claude Banon, responsible for Générale des Eaux's corporate development in the UK and US: 'We think there are very few [authorities] that would be interested in talking to us'.[24]

The water companies

For the statutory water companies, control by a French supplier is far from being the anathema it might at first appear. Their keenness (not, however, shared by the whole of the group) to be purchased by one of the trio (although the overtures of some are less welcome than others) reflects their fear of simply being swallowed up by neighbouring water plcs. This fear became all the more real in November 1988, when the then Secretary of State for the Environment, Nicholas Ridley, gave the green light to the water authorities to bid for the companies which work alongside them following flotation.[25] Later, of course, their unease abated somewhat, as the government's intention to preserve a sufficient number of companies for the purposes of comparison began to crystallise, thereby offering the beleaguered water companies some assurance of protection and respite. Uncertainty, however, remains. Governments are not known for their constancy, and particularly in an industry of such vital national importance, there is no guarantee that the rules of the game will not change, that the goal-posts will not shift at some unspecified time in the future.

Prior to flotation, the purchase of statutory water companies by water authorities had been discouraged by government on the grounds that public sector companies should not be allowed to use taxpayers' money to buy stakes in private companies. In June 1988, Nicholas Ridley referred the issue to the courts, after Northumbrian Water had purchased some small holdings, which it later sold. In December 1988, however, the High Court announced that it could see no reason whatsoever why a water authority should not take control of a water company.[26] But the government stuck to its guns, declaring itself to be 'reluctant and unlikely' to allow the authorities to raise further cash for share deals through any relaxation of their existing financial limits.[27] Political will remained strong, even without legal backing: several attempts by Southern Water to gain control of water companies in its area proved abortive.

But privatisation was to legitimise fund-raising by authorities. Suddenly the French 'predators' were seen by some of the statutory water companies in a new light, as 'white knights' to preserve them from engulfment. One of the smallest actually approached Générale des Eaux — generally recognised as the friendliest, most gentlemanly and least aggressive of the three — and asked to be bought over.

So are the private water companies simply caught 'between the devil and the deep blue sea'? Are the French merely the lesser of two undisputed evils, or does ownership by the French offer any specific additional advantages?

Ownership by the French offers the private water companies the major advantage of decentralised control, which means non-interference in the day-to-day running of the business.

When, in January 1989, Southern Water together with Associated Insurance Pension Fund lost the battle for Folkestone and District water company to Générale des Eaux, the company's former chairman, Sir John Arbuthnot, said that he strongly believed that the arm's-length approach adopted by the French would be the nearest thing to leaving local management intact.

The local management of one water company purchased by Générale des Eaux shortly before Christmas 1988, has indeed remained intact. Two non-executive directors nominated by the parent company joined the five existing executive directors in April 1989. So in a strict vote, the French nominees would clearly be outnumbered. But as the company's managing director emphasises: 'That is not how we do it — we don't take votes. We're concerned with working together'.[28] On major strategic issues, the opinions of board members nominated by the French parent clearly matter; but it is left to local managers to respond to local particularities. Financial issues — turnover, operating profit, the funding of local initiatives — are the concern of the French parent company; the daily running of the business is not. With this recipe of tight financial and loose operational control, Générale des Eaux achieves the last of the 'eight basics' of excellent management practice highlighted by Peters and Waterman (1982): that of simultaneous tight-loose properties, the coexistence of autonomy with central control. The benefit of this is that it makes the best use of individual expertise. Local managers are best equipped to deal with the coal-face of their own particular problem; central managers are best placed to judge the direction of the seam.

But these are early days, and while the French have promised to preserve the water companies' independence, this commitment has yet to be properly tested. If a subsidiary were to resist its parent's plans, top-down implementation of decisions taken in Paris might well prove to be forthcoming. One water authority chairman observes that the French are unlikely to leave to their own devices acquisitions for which they have paid more than £300 million all told. Where, moreover, does effective control begin? Probably before the official 30 per cent threshold. After all, it is a relatively easy matter for a shareholder with a 15-25 per cent stake in a British company to block proposals at the Annual General Meeting. Even companies which are not owned outright by the French may therefore be under their effective control. Bristol Water, for example, has nominally remained independent. But with Générale des Eaux and Lyonnaise des Eaux holding stakes in the company of 29 per cent and 18 per cent respectively, and with the two rivals now showing a new willingness to work together abroad (see above, Chapter 4), how much leverage does its local management actually have? To the water authority chairman mentioned above, style of independence is paramount; and he considers the French-controlled water companies to be little more than 'puppets to a puppet master'.[29]

Whatever their degree and style of independence, the French-owned water companies derive considerable fringe benefits from their association with the French. Benefits which include experience of competition, up-to-the-minute technology, and a welcome escape from the frustrations of British short-termism. The French are used to taking a long-term approach (the contracts they sign with the local municipalities in France often extend over three decades); and what is more, they can afford to do so. Générale des Eaux is one of the largest companies to be listed on the French Stock Exchange. So, through their liaison with the French, the small British water companies have access to financial resources which they could not otherwise have dreamt of.

With their conversion to plc status, French-owned water companies are encouraged to be innovative, to develop their own local ideas.[30] Business plans are to be submitted to the parent company, and, if approved, the necessary funds will be made available. According to the managing director of one water company, expansion and development are far simpler when one has a good relationship with a parent company than when one is obliged to satisfy a multiplicity of shareholders, blinkered perhaps by a short-term perspective, and anxious to earn a quick return on their investment. Whereas his proposal to start a trout farm in 1967 was rejected by shareholders, he is confident that his current plans will be approved.

Yet this managing director is also aware that the success of his company's relationship with Générale des Eaux depends crucially on the ability of everyone in the organisation to make the necessary culture jump: 'I myself have made it; but everyone needs to make it'.[31] The key to the successful functioning of a global network of local businesses lies ultimately in the assumption of a coherent culture. The creativity and entrepreneurship fostered by loose operational control are most productive when contained within an overarching discipline based on a small number of shared values (Peters and Waterman, 1982). Bournois and Chauchat (1990) found that a growing number of European companies are seeking to define an unchanging company culture which transcends individual national cultures.[32]

'Puppets to a puppet master' the water companies may be; but the traffic is far from being one-way. This same managing director has been invited to join the French board of a Générale des Eaux subsidiary in Paris. And he is confident that French and British can work together to mutual benefit. To this end one important initiative has already been taken. Générale des Eaux has set up a Franco-British research club known as GUSTO (General Utilities Scientific and Technical Organisation), which seeks to unite in a framework which nevertheless remains loose and flexible the technical and scientific competence of each of the nine British water companies in which Générale des Eaux has an interest together with the company's own Research and Development department, Anjou Recherche.

The benefit to shareholders: yesterday's windfalls and sunk costs?

The takeover bids from the French water suppliers succeeded because they made the shareholders of the statutory water companies an offer they simply could not refuse.

They were the real winners, those shareholders who took a stake in the private water companies in 1987. By Christmas 1988, their water company stock had increased in value more than fifteen times its purchase price.[33]

Yet it seems that the gains reaped by the shareholders of the past may be destined to remain yesterday's windfalls. Further, the enormous initial investment ploughed into the sector by the French may turn out to be little more than sunk costs. For it remains unclear whether the new French shareholders will be able to earn a satisfactory return on that investment. As outlined in Chapter 4, much depends upon the effect of the adjustment K factors issued to the private water companies by the DoE, and which in the event proved to be significantly lower than those accorded to the privatised water authorities. Equally, much depends on the ability of the new shareholders to access land value. If access to land value is not forthcoming, then the private water companies will have failed singularly to secure the 'level playing-field' they have consistently demanded. But without a level playing-field, it will be difficult to interest new investors in that sector of the industry. In this 'worst case' scenario, much would then depend on the water companies' ability to successfully diversify into other profit-making activities.

Shareholders of the privatised water authorities, by contrast, have little to fear. As French companies chased water shares on the first day of trading (12 December 1989), the 100 pence partly-paid share price escalated effortlessly to between 139 pence (for Severn-Trent) and 157 pence (for Northumbrian). In fact, UBS Phillips and Drew foresee 'substantial upside possibilities' for those who invest in the water plcs, with no downside (see above, Chapter 2). The water plcs' first year as listed companies appeared to confirm this. Despite a difficult year — two consecutive dry summers had severely depleted water resources, while the industry's image continued to suffer from the bad publicity generated by the Camelford poisoning incident and its ensuing court case — water stocks surged ahead, outperforming the rest of the market by an average of 34 per cent. Water shares offer a high yield coupled with all the advantages of an old-fashioned, regulated utility — a winning combination as the recession began to bite. For the water industry is not subject to the normal vagaries of business life. K guarantees steady price increases whatever the state of the economy, whatever the level of interest rates or inflation, while 'cost pass-through' ensures that unforeseen expenditure will not be met out of shareholders' dividends, whatever the environmental exigences of Brussels bureaucrats. And there is a very real sense in which the water plcs' market is truly captive. One cannot drop one's subscription to this particular firm simply because times are hard. Ultimately, consumers need water to survive.

To some extent, however, future gain may depend upon the perpetuation of 'cost pass-through', on unexpected costs, which were not accounted for in the K setting exercise, being passed on to the customer. But, as the *Financial Times* observes, no doubt the Director General of Water, Mr Ian Byatt, will do his best to please: after all, his counterpart at Ofgas has demonstrated by example that 'a privatised utility has a duty to its shareholders to exploit its monopoly position', if only to the limits of propriety and prudence.[34]

The customer's fate: Hobson's choice?

Whether the French are in or out is unlikely to make much difference to the customer, for whom the outlook is unmitigatingly bleak. Charges will escalate throughout the remainder of this century, irrespective of the French involvement. Nicholas Ridley's estimate of a 7.5 per cent to 12.5 per cent annual increase in real terms in the decade following the privatisation of the industry, is likely to be a risible underestimate.[35] One of the justifications for privatisation frequently cited is that needed investment will be financed more easily by private capital than from the constraints of the public expenditure budget. Yet it is the customer who will have to pay in higher charges for a better return on capital than the 5 per cent in real terms used in the state sector.[36]

Water company prices rose by an average of 22 per cent in 1989, to help bring them up to the charging levels of most of the former authorities. It would seem that this exorbitant price rise may be the sour taste of things to come. The mechanism of 'cost pass-through' ensures that consumers — rather than shareholders — bear the brunt of any unforeseen costs which may arise. Yet the principle of 'cost pass-through' is not entirely in tune with the ethos which evolved in the 1980s, the same ethos on which Mrs Thatcher's flagship, the ill-fated and electorally unpopular 'poll tax' was based: namely that one should pay for the services one uses. As Bowers et al. (1989) point out, 'The consumer might reasonably be expected to meet the cost of drinking water quality improvements since she is receiving the benefits, but not the cost of improvements in coastal waters and river quality. She is neither the principal beneficiary nor the direct cause of the problem'.[37] Moreover, with the abolition of the rateable value charging system and the advent of the council tax, the banded property tax which owes something to both the old rates system and the poll tax which it speedily replaced,[38] universal metering is imminent, boosting the sales of flow meter manufacturers at customers' expense. Large families have most to fear from the arrival of measured consumption. But as the management of Générale des Eaux underlines, unmeasured water is not necessarily the best way to redistribute national wealth: 'That is another problem. We're not a charity. We're not there to do social work'.[39]

But the privatisation of water, from which the French are set to benefit, has been an costly operation, eating up more than £8 billion of taxpayers' money, each of whom is also a customer. *Financial Times* columnist Lex describes the taxpayer as the 'chief dupe' of the City's 'three-card trick': 'Chief dupe looks like being the taxpayer, who will net only around £500 million as first payment on an industry which had assets of £7.7 billion even on a limited historic cost accounting basis'.[40] Those taxpayers who are not also shareholders will reap no benefit from this enormous expenditure. As Bishop and Kay argue in their study of privatisation in the UK, 'expenditures occurred in privatisation represent in part a waste of resources and in part *a transfer of them from the rest of the population — the population which pays taxes but does not buy shares*' (my stress).[41] Assurances from the Director General of Water that his first duty is 'to ensure that the consumer does not pay more for water than is necessary' is likely to bring cold comfort; for how he will do this as the hands-off, arm's-length regulator he has vowed to be (see above, Chapter 3) is unclear.[42]

Unions and employees

When Lyonnaise des Eaux first began to make inroads into the British water market, and both Générale des Eaux and SAUR looked set to follow suit, and when it became clear that their joint intentions were to provide a whole range of additional municipal services, union officials at the public service union NALGO (the National Association of Local Government Officials), the largest trade union in the industry, and NUPE (National Union of Public Employees) were understandably alarmed. With the cooperation of the French communist-dominated labour union, the Confédération Générale du Travail (CGT) in Paris, they investigated the long-term financial aims of the French, assisted by French laws which oblige companies to divulge investment policies.

In general, the union delegates concerned returned relatively reassured from their visit. While Ron Keating, assistant general secretary of NUPE retained some reservations,[43] NALGO reached the overall conclusion that 'these companies offered the only means for private capital to be invested in the water industry'.[44] They also appreciated the long-term nature of these investments: the French were clearly not out to make a quick buck at the workers' expense. All three companies had professed their confidence in existing management teams, without concealing their intentions to place a small numbers of representatives on water company Boards. (Lyonnaise des Eaux emerged as the most aggressive of the three in this respect, revealing its intention to take seats on Boards wherever it could.) Both Lyonnaise des Eaux and Générale des Eaux were keen to promote employee sharehold-ings, with the latter in favour of inviting employee representatives to Board meetings, as is the practice in France in accordance with French labour law. Interestingly, however, while NALGO has come to recognise the general legitimacy of French purchases of British water companies, the union has consistently opposed stake-building by water authorities as an abuse of taxpayers' money.

It seems that the British employees of French-owned statutory water com-panies *do* stand to gain from the French involvement. The jobs of work-ers and managers alike are more secure with the French, who can effec-tively shield them from the predatory advances of neighbouring water plcs, should these be forthcoming. 'We need local people to operate our services', one CGE top manager assured in a personal interview. When Southern Wa-ter was thwarted in its bids for West Kent and Mid-Sussex water companies by SAUR, the French advantage derived partly from fears that amalgama-tion with the authority would lead to job losses.[45] This Southern virulently denied. Yet it is difficult to see what overriding motive for rationalisation there could be, other than that of the efficiency gains which would result from economies of scale realised partly through manpower reductions.[46] With little scope for efficiency gains by water plcs now remaining follow-ing the considerable achievements of the 1980s, this particular means of improving performance might well prove to be irresistible. In June 1990, Yorkshire Water announced the loss of 200 jobs through voluntary redun-dancies as one of its management tiers was removed — the necessary price, according to chairman Gordon Jones, of getting the company closer to its customers.[47]

By the same token, however, the failure to realise these potential econ-omies of scale — which both French ownership and the upholding of the principle of 'comparative competition' seem to imply — signifies in turn an opportunity loss for the customer. As Joel Dean (1951) underlines: 'What the firm is *not* doing but *could* do is frequently the critical cost consideration which it is perilous but easy to ignore'.[48]

The environment

The sound and fury which surrounded the privatisation of water in the UK was fuelled by its unfortunate timing, occurring as it did at a time when an environmentally naïve British public was taking a major first step towards environmental awareness. Some idea of the growth of public con-cern about the environment can be gleaned from the surge in membership of green groups during the 1980s, with membership of Friends of the Earth in England and Wales increasing sevenfold (from 18,000 in 1981 to 140,000 in 1989), while that of the World Wildlife Fund trebled (from 60,000 at the beginning of the decade to 200,000 by the end).[49] This new concern was bound to impact on public attitudes to water. Suddenly, Britain's dirty beaches and substandard drinking water were an issue of national—and European—significance. Given the overriding importance of the issues at stake, it is legitimate to ask whether French ownership of British water is likely to enhance or impede British compliance with EC directives on water quality. A separate chapter examines and compares the track record of Britain and France on water quality.

Summary of conclusions

The present chapter reviews the balance sheet of the French penetration of British water for the principal stakeholders concerned. Overall, this is believed to be positive.

While the presence of French competitors on the doorstep of newly privatised water authorities may well disrupt the latter's plans, it forces a strategy overhaul on to their agenda; and there has never been competitive advantage without competition. These fully diversified French companies provide a useful model of what may be achieved. Yet the key potential benefit offered by the French suppliers is unlikely to be exploited by the water plcs: the French desire for partnerships with the British may well remain unfulfilled.

French ownership offers the statutory water companies the advantage of decentralised control: the nearest thing, perhaps, to leaving local management intact. There are additional fringe benefits: experience of competition, up-to-date technology, welcome relief from British short-termism, and substantial financial backing for local initiatives. If the style and degree of independence accorded to local management is open to question, this is certainly not a case of one-way traffic: a Franco-British research club has already been set up by Générale des Eaux for mutual profitability. But the gains reaped by shareholders of the past may be destined to remain yesterday's windfalls, and the huge initial investment by the French may turn out to be little more than sunk costs, should the value of water company stock plummet in response to water company K figures, which in the event were lower than expected. The outlook for the customer is unmitigatingly bleak: exorbitant price rises would seem to be the sour taste of things to come. For water company employees, however, the French provide a measure of job security through the protection they afford from the predatory advances of neighbouring water plcs (in the not unlikely event that the rules of the game are changed) or their own suppliers. A separate chapter examines whether French ownership of British water is likely to enhance or impede British compliance with EC directives on water quality.

Notes

1.   See 'Yesterday's windfalls', *Financial Times*, Supplement on Water, 25 November 1989, p. X.

2.   On resistance to change, see Ansoff, I., op. cit., pp. 235–42.

3.   Porter, M. E., 'How competitive forces shape strategy', *Harvard Business Review*, March-April 1979.

4.   Ownership of Lyonnaise des Eaux-Dumez at the time of the merger in July 1990 was as follows: institutional investors and members of the public: 61.6 per cent; the Chaufour family (including the company Sogepar) 10 per cent; the powerful insurance firm Union des Assurances de Paris (UAP): 6.6 per cent; the nationalised bank Crédit Lyonnais: 4.1 per cent; company personnel 2.5 per cent; Sociedad General de Agua de Barcelona: 1.7 per cent; the privatised electricity giant Compagnie Générale d'Eléctricité: 1.5 per cent. See 'Le groupe Lyonnaise des eaux-Dumez représente un chiffre d'affaires de 82 milliards de francs', op. cit.

5.   During the second five years, higher levels of foreign ownership are to be allowed, on condition that 75 per cent of the shareholders of the company concerned approve.

6.   See 'Three statutory water companies plan merger', *Financial Times*, 28 July 1989, p. 26.

7.   The 1980s saw land prices spiral in the South East. They rose by 27.3 per cent in the year to April 1986, by which time the average price of land in the area (according to the National Council of Building Material Producers) was within the range £684,000-892,000 per hectare. Source: Key Note Publications (1987), *The Housebuilding Industry*.

8.   General Utilities has full control of Lee Valley, and holdings of 28.2 per cent and 16.1 per cent in Colne Valley and Rickmansworth respectively (see above, Chapter 4). Altogether its stake in Three Valleys could be as much as 50 per cent.

9.   See 'Government blocks planned water company merger', *Independent*, 28 April 1990, p. 23.

10. Personal interview with the author, July 1989, Paris.

11. See Miles, R. E. and Snow, C. C. (1978), *Organizational Strategy, Structure and Process*, McGraw-Hill, Toronto.

12. Ohmae, K. (1987), *The Mind of the Strategist: the art of Japanese business*, Penguin, Harmondsworth, p. 36.

13. See for example 'Refreshing water in year of horrors', *Independent on Sunday*, 6 January 1991, p. 18.

14. See Chapman, C., op. cit., pp. 45–7.

15. Personal interview with the author, June 1989.

16. See Ohmae, K. (1990), 'Global logic of strategic alliances', *EuroBusiness*, vol. 2, no. 2, p. 18. This article forms part of a chapter in Ohmae's recent book *The*

Borderless World: power and strategy in the interlinked economy (1990), Collins, London.

17. Cited in 'Storming the barricade', *The Economist*, 14 October 1989, p. 46.
18. ibid.
19. Cited in Ohmae, K., 'The Global logic of strategic alliances', op. cit., p. 18.
20. Sharp, M. and Shearman, C., op. cit., p. 100.
21. See 'Why a French supplier is bubbling with enthusiasm for British water', op. cit.
22. Personal interview with the author, June 1989.
23. One top manager at Générale des Eaux specified the lack of linguistic skills on the part of UK water plcs as a key handicap to their winning contracts abroad. Personal interview, July 1989, Paris.
24. Quoted in 'French water company may seek privatisation partnerships', *Financial Times*, 8 August 1989, p. 8.
25. See 'Ridley gives green light to water tie-ups', *Financial Times*, 25 November 1988, p. 19.
26. See 'Court clears way for UK water takeovers', *Financial Times*, 22 December 1988, p. 1.
27. See 'Government to discourage water takeovers', *Financial Times*, 3 January 1989, p. 7.
28. Personal interview with the author, July 1989.
29. Personal interview with the author, June 1989.
30. The 29 statutory water companies are now able to free themselves from their restrictions, and, with shareholder approval, may convert to public limited company status. One of the first to do so was Mid Kent water company, which, in March 1989, became Mid Kent Holdings. But not all may choose to convert. For those which remain independent to date, and whose voting rights are restricted, the conversion to plc status carries with it the unwelcome threat of takeover.
31. Personal interview with the author, July 1989.
32. See Bournois, F. and Chauchat, J-H, op. cit., p. 7.
33. See 'Yesterday's windfalls', op. cit.
34. Cited in 'If you see Sid, commiserate', op. cit.
35. See 'Charges may rise 12.5 per cent in decade', *Financial Times*, 29 November 1988, p. 18.
36. See 'State control over water', *Financial Times*, 25 November 1988, p. 12
37. Bowers, J. et al. (1989), *Liquid Costs*, op. cit., p. 4.
38. Unmeasured charges are currently applied to the vast majority of households and some commercial establishments. They are generally on a two-part basis: a fixed standing charge, accounting on average for 25 per cent of the total, plus a charge per pound of domestic rateable value. Water plcs will not be allowed to use rateable values to calculate charges after the year 2000.

39. Personal interview with the author, July 1989, Paris.
40. Cited in Chapman, C., op. cit., p. 40.
41. Cited in 'Privatisation as an end in itself', op. cit.
42. Cited in 'Treasury man to direct water services', *Financial Times*, 5 April 1989, p. 8.
43. See 'French giants eye up UK water industry', *Independent*, 8 October 1988, p. 21.
44. Cited in NALGO (1988), *Report on NALGO's delegation to the French Water Industry*, p. 1.
45. Reported in 'Battle for West Kent Water', *Financial Times*, 20 January 1989, p. 23.
46. The efficiency gains achieved by the industry in the 1980s were realised largely through manpower reductions. See UBS Phillips and Drew, op. cit., p. 24.
47. See 'Yorkshire Water to make 200 redundant', *Independent*, 30 June 1990, p. 21.
48. See Dean, J. (1951), *Managerial Economics*, Prentice-Hall International, Hemel Hempstead.
49. Reported in 'Membership surges in "green" groups', *Independent*, 17 January 1991, p. 9.

6 Perceptions of Quality: Britain, France and water

Milton! thou shouldst be living at this hour:
England hath need of thee: she is a fen
Of stagnant waters — (Wordsworth).

The planet strikes back

Among the most emotive issues in the great water sell-off was the perceived threat to the environment.

Water is not just *any* product: it is essential to life. And while quality — quality of product and quality of life — is tipped to be of increasing importance to European Community consumers in the 1990s (along with individualism, luxury and convenience), the quality of this *particular* product is a vital determinant of public health.[1] It is also crucially dependent on the cleanliness (or degradation) of our environment.

The reason why the private water companies of London were taken over by the Metropolitan Water Board in the nineteenth century was because water supply is more than just a utility: it has the potential for spreading disease. The reforming Acts of the nineteenth and twentieth centuries had, in providing Britons with a clean water supply and monitoring sewage effluent, as big an impact on public health as all the medical breakthroughs throughout the same period. Cholera and typhoid were all but eliminated; dysentery, hepatitis and gastro-enteritis became much rarer.

Yet those who believe that this disease-spreading potential is firmly a thing of the past, in the UK if not in the Third World (where it is estimated that one child dies every three seconds from illness caused by contaminated water)[2], need only consider the Camelford poison case of 1988. Twenty thousand people in north Cornwall fell ill after twenty tons of aluminium sulphate were accidentally tipped into a water tank at the Lowermoor treatment works, and thence into their drinking water supply.[3] According to independent experts, brain damage and memory loss resulted (although the

91

official Clayton report commissioned by the Department of Health played down the ill effects, attributing the widespread sickness endured by victims to anxiety rather than physical causes).[4] The French interpreted this as proof that their expertise was badly needed across the Channel: 'Another telling sign of the poor functioning of water distribution in the UK', wrote the French daily *Le Monde*.[5]

If the infectious disease problems of Victorian times have been largely overcome, today's problems are far more sophisticated in nature. For the synthetic chemicals and other dangerous substances which have become ubiquitous in our environment are menacing us with chronic diseases resulting from long-term exposure to trace contaminants (Okun, 1986).

It is known, for instance, that the slow leaching of nitrates into the water supply in the Anglian region may trigger 'blue baby syndrome'. This is caused by the reaction of nitrate in the bloodstream with haemoglobin, the oxygen-carrying constituent of red blood cells, to produce methaemoglobin which cannot transport oxygen, of which the victim is thus starved.[6]

It is similarly known that lead piping in Scotland contributes to brain damage in children, harming their intelligence and giving rise to hyperactivity and restlessness. Drinking water supplies in Dumfries and Galloway, Fife, Grampian, Highland, Lothian, Strathclyde and Tayside regions infringe the EC safety limit of 50 micrograms of lead per litre, according to an EC report. The British government considers up to 100 micrograms of lead per litre to be 'safe'; but even by this relaxed standard, seventy-eight of Scotland's water supplies are admitted by the Scottish office to exceed safety limits.

It is suspected that nitrate, converted to nitrite in the body, may react with other substances in the stomach to bring about cancer.[7]

It is similarly suspected that high levels of aluminium in drinking water in Yorkshire lead to senile dementia in old people (as high levels of the element coupled with low levels of calcium and magnesium cause nerve cell fibres in the brain to tangle and knot). The importance of Alzheimer's disease is increasing as Western populations age; the annual death toll in the United States alone is already 120,000.

The ill effects of other, man-made substances in our water supply — such as pesticides, or the suspected carcinogens, trihalomethanes — may be tomorrow's grisly discovery. May 1991 saw the publication of the results of a joint NRA, MAFF and Greenpeace investigation into marine life in the heavily-polluted Mersey estuary. Seals were found to have been rendered sterile by blockages and malformations of the womb, thought to be caused by PCBs (polychlorinated biphenyls). Meanwhile, tests carried out by Liverpool University on 50 dolphins, seals and porpoises found dead on the shores of the Irish Sea found that a quarter had died of pneumonia, with PCBs again the principal suspect, thought to have destroyed their immune system.[8] One tenth of Britain's groundwater supplies are believed to contain cancer-inducing solvents which exceed the limits recommended by the World Health Organisation.[9]

Until more research has been done, and until more time has elapsed, however, we are likely to be kept in the dark as to precisely how pure water needs to be,[10] and about much else besides. Significantly, while the government admitted that fish in the Mersey estuary and elsewhere in British waters was unfit for human consumption, it nevertheless refused to say which fishing grounds were contaminated.

And yet how fitting is it that we should play a waiting game, attendant on absolute proof, while the nitrate time-bomb ticks away, eventually to explode? The greatest achievement of Environment Secretary Chris Patten during his term in office was to persuade the former prime minister Margaret Thatcher to accept at long last the 'precautionary principle' with regard to the particular instance of sewage dumping at sea. The precautionary principle maintains that although no clear cause-effect relationship between sludge dumping and environmental deterioration has as yet been proven, any damage might be irreparable were governments to sit around waiting for conclusive results. Should not this principle be applied to other aspects of the environment? How appropriate is it, for instance, that individual householders should be held responsible for the lead piping on their properties when the mental health of the nation's children — the country's future — is at stake? So far-reaching a consideration is surely beyond the remit of any single private limited company. As Joseph Chamberlain argued in 1894 with respect to water, 'It is difficult and indeed almost impossible to reconcile the rights and interests of the public with the claims of an individual company seeking as its material and legitimate object the largest private gain'.[11] Is there not a sense in which government has abdicated its responsibilities in this domain, foisting them on to the private sector in the hope that market forces will suffice?

The English librettist W. S. Gilbert once wrote that 'Man is Nature's sole mistake'. There is a Greenpeace manifesto which likens the four-thousand, six-hundred-million year-old planet Earth to a person of 46 years of age. According to this time-scale, modern man has existed for only four hours, and the industrial revolution began but a minute ago:

> During those sixty seconds, [man] has made a rubbish tip of Paradise. He has multiplied his numbers to plague proportions, caused the extinction of 500 species of animals, ransacked the planet for fuels and now stands like a brutish infant, gloating over this meteoric rise to ascendancy, on the brink of effectively destroying this oasis of life in the solar system.[12]

By this time frame, only for the merest fraction of a second has man dared to contemplate that 'mute Nature' might not forgive him his worst excesses. In 1982, Fritjof Capra wrote that 'the global ecosystem and the further evolution of life on earth are seriously endangered and may well end in a large ecological disaster'.[13] Now, with 3,000 acres of rainforest destroyed each month, it seems that we may be nearing the point of no return. New global threats — ozone depletion and greenhouse warming, triggering violent storms and severe droughts, causing polar ice to melt and sea-levels to rise — are our strongest warnings yet that we must clean up our act, or be damned. Unless this path on which we as human beings have embarked is replaced by another, more concerned with the future habitability of the planet, then according to World Wildlife Fund predictions, changes in our climate may destroy vast areas, causing plants and animals to become extinct at an estimated rate of 100 per day. In August 1990 the Intergovernmental Panel on Climate Change, composed of more than 300 scientists from more than 20 nations, concluded after two years of careful investigation that unless urgent steps were taken to combat the greenhouse effect, the world's climate was on course to become hotter than at any time in the previous two million years. Harvests will fail; a quarter of a million miles of the coastline will disappear; tens of millions of unfortunates will be homeless; and tropical diseases will spread into more temperate climates, including southern Europe.[14]

The European Community has been concerned with protecting the environment since its inception. Yet, as we saw in Chapter 2, there has been some debate as to whether the environmental legislation of the Treaty of Rome (1957) was in fact congruent with other provisions of the treaty (Haigh, 1987). The amendment of the treaty on 1 July 1987 by the Single European Act, however, has given a clear basis for legal actions by the Community relating to the environment. Henceforth, measures for protecting the environment shall be fully integrated with the Community's other policies.[15]

The 1980s have been termed the 'Green decade' — they have seen the Green parties of Europe step out of the political sidelines on to centre stage. By 1989, there were Green representatives serving on eight of the twelve national parliaments of the Community, and their ideas were being increasingly co-opted by mainstream European parties, as politicians tried to jump on the environmental train as it gathered momentum, having done little or nothing to get it out of the station in the first place. In the European elections of June 1989 the Greens polled 15 per cent of the vote[16] — a reflection of widespread public concern that we may be losing the battle to protect our natural habitat. Indeed perhaps, as Tom Birch argues, all we have achieved in the 1980s is to recognise that the battle has to be fought in the first place: 'All that we have done in this last decade is to recognize that [environmental problems] require political solutions. But that is simply to arrive at the starting gate. We have yet to get going'.[17]

Every green issue represents a trade-off between the damage that might be caused by continuing to make or emit a particular poison, and the constraint on economic growth of stopping it. But while in the past national governments have tended to be concerned with damage limitation — except where they were the recipients of *another country's* pollution, when objections became more vociferous — national governments are now beginning to realise that the issues at stake are much more far-reaching than was originally thought. Called into question is the sustainability (or otherwise) of economic growth *vis-à-vis* the sustainability (or otherwise) of life on earth. Whether man's ingenuity will make sustainable growth possible, or whether growth will have to be contained in the interest of preserving the earth for mankind, may well prove to be the key political question of the twenty-first century.[18]

It is against this backcloth that the recent Commission crack-down on several member states for failing to comply with the 1980 directive on drinking water quality (80/778/EEC), despite a five-year period of grace, must be viewed. The purpose of the directive is twofold. On the one hand, it aims to protect human health; on the other, it aims to protect the environment.

Given the overriding importance of the issues at stake, it is legitimate to ask whether French ownership of British water is likely to enhance or impede British compliance with EC directives on water quality. The present chapter therefore examines and compares the track record of Britain and France on water quality; but with two provisos. First, this is a book about water companies rather than one whose primary concern is the environment. Readers who wish to know more about environmental quality are referred to Rose (1990), *The Dirty Man of Europe* and Haigh (1987), *EEC Environmental Policy and Britain*, both excellent and highly informative works. Second, the act of comparing is flawed from the outset when what is being compared is — perhaps to a large extent — not comparable: two different countries endowed with different resources, histories, business practices and government responsibilities. But if there are lessons to be learned from the French water companies, then the task may perhaps be worthwhile.

The quest for quality

But first, what is quality? — and how is it to be defined? Straightforward comparison of the quality of French and British water supplies is problematic because quality largely eludes definition.

Traditionally, quality has been measured — insofar as the qualitative can be quantified — by the transaction price of the finished goods or services: the amount people are prepared to pay for them (Handy, 1976). So more expensive goods and services are thought to reflect their better quality. At the same time, for the company concerned quality is often said to be free, since the cost of building more quality into a product can easily be recouped through savings in, say, after-sales servicing, as well as through

the premium price which customers are willing to pay (Crosby, 1979).[19]
The premium price of Stella Artois lager becomes an advertisement for its
superior quality: Stella, we are told, is 'reassuringly expensive'.

In the water industry, however, benefit cannot be measured in monetary
terms. The output of the water industry — the benefits perceived by consumers — are measured through the level of service indicators.[20] Nor is it
free: the improvements exacted by EC directives on water quality — and
there are more directives on water than on any other aspect of the environment — may come at high marginal cost for what may prove to be but
marginal gain (see above, Chapter 4).

But while we may try to pin quality down by, say, level of service indicators, quality is also a function of the wealth of any society, of its expectations, its taste, and the sophistication of its technology. As such it is a
relative concept rather than an absolute one, contingent upon external factors. For example, when 'Anaïs', a new bottom-of-the-range *eau de toilette*
from the French perfumer L'Oréal failed to sell, the company deemed that
cosmetic changes alone were necessary. It doubled the price, sold the product in more exclusive outlets, spent more on packaging, changed the name
of both product (to 'Anaïs Anaïs') and manufacturer (to Cacharel, which it
had recently acquired), and sales soared. Dreams, it appears, cannot be sold
cheaply. The French company Bic learned a similar lesson. The company's
attempt to repeat the success of its throwaway pens and disposable razors
with a touch of class on the cheap — £2 perfumes, sold in supermarkets in
plain glass bottles — was abandoned after three years of stagnating sales
and heavy losses.[21]

Two lessons emerge from the above. First, price is far from being a fool-
proof measure of quality — so the fact that French water is more expensive
than British water does not necessarily mean that it is better. Second, and
more importantly, *image* has an important role to play in forming customers'
perceptions of the product being purchased: quality is to some extent in
the eye of the beholder.

The quality of water

Britain once defined clean water simply as 'wholesome' (and some of her
private water companies still do). But how water quality is defined is also a
function of scientific and technological advancement, depending as it does
on the sensitivity and sophistication of sampling equipment and proce-
dures. With the agreement of the EC directive on drinking water quality in
1980, this simple definition of pure water made a major leap in complexity,
giving way to another comprised of sixty-six parameters which could be
measured and quantified by specified guide levels, maximum admissible
concentrations or minimum required concentrations. These parameters are

grouped into six categories as follows:

1. organoleptic parameters, covering colour, odour, taste;
2. physiochemical parameters, e.g. pH balance, conductivity;
3. parameters concerning substances undesirable in excessive amounts, such as nitrates, nitrites;
4. parameters concerning toxic substances, such as mercury, lead, pesticides;
5. microbiological parameters — coliforms, faecal streptococci;
6. minimum required concentration for softened water intended for human consumption, e.g. hardness, alkalinity (Haigh, 1987).

In the eyes of the Commission, drinking water is clean when, according to the above criteria, it is 100 per cent pure at the tap 100 per cent of the time.

This, however, is a point of contention. British water chiefs believe that so absolute an approach may lead to very high water charges for not very worthwhile improvements, and that a more flexible approach to drinking water standards should be adopted. They also insist that the tools of analysis now available are so powerful that to conform with all of the standards all of the time is practically impossible.[22] For British water suppliers, who would prefer a 95 per cent target, 100 per cent compliance is rendered all the more difficult in that piping from the mains in the street to the tap in the home is not regarded as their responsibility. Lead found in tap-water, for example, is more likely to come from pipes on the premises than from the water supply itself.[23] The French suppliers agree that the norms set by the Commission are 'too stringent'.[24] One water authority chairman claimed that the French had admitted to him that if any sample taken did not satisfy the directive, they simply kept on sampling until they obtained one that did![25]

Nevertheless, Lyonnaise des Eaux has made quality (of product and service) one of its key organisational goals. The group recognises that success depends upon the *internalisation* of this objective by the entirety of the workforce: 'Quality is first and foremost the translation of a daily commitment on the part of 40,000 men and women always to strive for a better service'.[26] The internalisation of any objective depends in turn on its effective *communication*: people have to understand what is expected of them (Merchant, 1985). To this end a company meeting was held in 1988, attended by all echelons of management. The point here is that the internalisation of a quality objective is likely to mould internal perceptions — and hence the *identity* — of the organisation. This is a crucial first step if others are to be persuaded to believe in the *quality image* the company is seeking to foster. The view of Peters and Waterman (1982) is that a 100 per cent quality programme can be made to succeed through *faith*. In the excellent companies,

they claim, the impossible becomes possible and a 100 per cent quality programme therefore plausible: 'If you don't shoot for one hundred percent,
you are tolerating mistakes. You'll get what you asked for'.[27] The message
here would seem to be this: if you believe you can do it, you might just
make it; but if you don't believe in yourself, don't expect anyone else to
either.

Sticking to EC rules: Britain, France and other member states

Both Britain and France play the rules of compliance reasonably well. On
the implementation of the 68 internal market directives which should have
become national law in all twelve states by the time of the privatisation
of water in 1989, France was at the head of the league table of compliance
(54 implemented, 8 not implemented, 1 infringement), with Britain coming a
respectable fourth (50 implemented, 11 not implemented, 1 infringement).[28]
If the 1980s are taken as a whole, and if the implementation of EC legislation in general together with the rulings of the European Court of Justice
are taken into consideration, then Britain can truly claim to be a 'good European'. Only Denmark has a better record, and some of the more overtly
pro-European and integrationist member states, Italy and Belgium included,
emerge rather poorly in this respect.[29]

Directive 80/778/EEC on drinking water quality was translated into
French national law — admittedly belatedly — on 3 January 1989, together
with directives 75/440/EEC and 79/869/EEC on surface water for drinking
and sampling methods respectively.[30] Britain, on the other hand, has been
accused by the Commission of failing to incorporate it fully into UK legislation, and as a result actions have been brought by the Commission against
the UK before the European Court of Justice on this and two other charges:
those of unauthorised levels of lead in Scotland, and high nitrate concentration in Norfolk and South Staffordshire.[31] The timetable for achieving full
compliance proved a further thorn, with the European Commission putting
pressure on Britain to satisfy the 66 different standards laid down by the
directive by 1993 at the latest, and Britain insisting that earlier than 1995 —
ten years after the elapsing of the original deadline — was unrealistic.

With such a complex and exacting directive, however, it would be ex-
traordinary if Britain were alone in her failure to comply. That the British
government has shown a distinct lack of regard for EC standards on water
purity is undeniable; yet other countries have done little better. 'Italy gets
away with blue murder', the general manager of one water company told
me. 'There are poor standards similarly in Spain and Greece, and a lack
of compliance in all EC member states'.[32] One water authority chairman
agreed: 'They call us the "dirty man" of Europe, but in fact we're the "clean
man" of Europe'.[33] Michael Howard, the minister responsible for steering
water privatisation through Parliament, claimed that there was no evidence

that others in Europe were doing more to comply with the standards than the British.[34] Environment Secretary Chris Patten went even further, maintaining that he knew of no other member state to have prepared 'such a rigorous, comprehensive and fully funded programme'.[35] According to the *Financial Times*, France and Belgium are also being taken to the European Court of Justice over their alleged violation of the drinking water directive, with Denmark and the former West Germany receiving reasoned opinions, and a second action being taken against Italy for the high concentrations of two pesticides (atrazine and molinate) in drinking water. Meanwhile, France, Belgium, Denmark, West Germany, the Netherlands, Ireland, Spain, and the UK, have received letters from the Commission concerning alleged bathing water violations.[36]

To what extent is this hearsay evidence corroborated by research findings? Recently published Community-wide research on the working of European policies at grass roots level (Butt Philip, 1989; Commission of the European Communities, 1988; Siedentopf and Ziller, 1988), does not accord much emphasis to those EC measures which concern the protection of the natural environment, perhaps because they are relatively new.[37] Nevertheless, the *Fifth Annual Report to the European Parliament on Commission monitoring of the application of Community law* (1987) *does* confirm that a large number of complaints concerning the quality of drinking and bathing water have been received from all corners of the Community.[38]

It would seem, then, that drinking water in the UK is not necessarily any worse than in France, nor anywhere else in Europe for that matter. The source of the furore over water quality in the UK probably lies elsewhere. At play here is likely to be the British government's decision to grant immunity from prosecution over environmental pollution to the new water plcs, provided they were doing all that the government deemed appropriate to comply.[39] In the eyes of the EC Environment Commissioner, Carlo Ripa di Meana, this was nothing less that a usurpation of EC law. This explains in part his somewhat curious statement that he hoped the court action would have a 'profound moral effect' on the errant UK.[40]

'Clean man' or 'dirty man' of Europe? — the importance of altering images

Certainly, levels of lead in Scotland and nitrates in Humberside and East Anglia are unacceptable. Granted, an intolerably high proportion of Britain's sewers are crumbling and dilapidated. In an industry overburdened with debt (until the recent debt write-off by government), relining and replacement programmes have been grossly inadequate to the country's actual requirements. The tightening of the strings of the national purse by successive governments has clearly meant sailing ever closer to the wind on levels of service indicators. As many as 1,074 sewage treatment works in England and Wales (more than a sixth of the total number) are unable to meet the standards laid down by the 'consent conditions' under which they are supposed to operate[41] — and this in spite of the fact that these very consent conditions had often been relaxed so that they might appear to be attained. As Chris Rose writes, 'To avoid the embarrassment of being prosecuted for failing to meet their own standards, the Water Authorities were encouraged by government to apply for weaker standards ('relaxed consents'). By 1986, 1,800 sewage works became dirtier, legally'.[42] River quality has similarly deteriorated.[43] Whereas five-yearly surveys of the quality of Britain's rivers registered a steady improvement from 1958– 80, of 37,911 kilometres of rivers examined in England and Wales in the five years from 1980 to 1985, 5,437 declined in standard, while only 4,489 showed an improvement.[44] Too many of Britain's beaches are spoilt when all too often raw sewage is washed back up on to the shore. The bathing water at some of Britain's most popular seaside resorts (including Blackpool, Morecombe, Cromer, Seaford, Ramsgate, Folkestone, Mounts Bay Penzance, Lyme Regis, New Haven and Herne Bay) is in breach of EC safety standards. And in 1988 pollution of water courses by British farmers reached record levels while prosecutions fell[45] — an indication less of declining standards than of woefully inadequate staffing levels at a demoralised Inspectorate of Pollution, where resignations had been rife.[46] Clearly, there is much work to be done if the British water industry is to shake off its image as the 'dirty man' of Europe — particularly since, according to industry chiefs, that image accords ill with the reality of the situation.

In a letter addressed to MPs in March 1989, the ten water authority chairmen attacked the welter of 'misinformation' which had falsified the truth about the industry and concealed its real achievements *vis-à-vis* those of other EC member states. An information sheet attached to the letter stressed the following points:

1. 92 per cent of rivers in the UK and 66 per cent in England and Wales are in class one [according to the National Water Council four-class system for grading rivers, see note 44], compared with 39 per cent in Europe overall.

2. 67 per cent of Britain's 389 identified beaches comply with EC requirements, and the remainder will do so by 1995.

3. 96 per cent of the UK population is connected to a sewer: a percentile unequalled by any other member state.[47]

The letter observed that difficulties in attaining EC quality requirements were by no means unique to Britain, but were common to all European countries.

France's difficulties include inadequate provision against drought, particularly in the South West.[48] There is the high cost of irrigation, accounting for as much as 35 per cent of water bills, and which, again, is especially vital in the arid South West. River quality has generally deteriorated. The clean-up of the Thames — which now boasts salmon, mullet, flounder as well as eels, and which, while still vulnerable, is nevertheless much cleaner in its middle reaches than it was some 50 years ago — is extolled as an example of what might be achieved with the Seine.[49] Substandard drinking water continues to be supplied to one quarter of the 33 million inhabitants of rural areas.[50] As little as one third (35 per cent) of dirty water from French households is purified.[51] Raw sewage is discharged into the Mediterranean.[52] Drinking water is often laced with nitrate and pesticides (France is the most heavily farmed country of the Community), a problem which has become more severe with the summer droughts of recent years, as toxins become more concentrated.[53]

Yet at least in France these problems are being tackled from the top, whether or not the bulk of the industry is in private hands. The French government responded to the droughts of the late 1980s by seeking to define a coherent policy for water management in the short, medium and long term.[54] Water featured prominently in the Green Plan drawn up by Environment Minister Brice Lalonde. If, in the UK, the government has removed itself from the vital process of managing a national resource, the French government ensures a continuing long-term perspective and an enduring responsibility, ready to intervene if necessary to correct the short-sightedness and short-termism of individual firms and markets.

The above difficulties, however, are only part of the story. The public relations skills of the French water suppliers are such that it is their *good side* which is almost exclusively projected. So they are better known for their great strides in research, for their contribution to scientific progress in water services and treatment, and even for making France a world leader in these techniques (Malandain and Tavernier, 1991). Lyonnaise des Eaux, for instance, has recently developed a treatment plant which, by means of new 'membrane' technology, purifies dirty water without recourse to chemicals. The French suppliers are up-front about landmark achievements, such as the honour conferred upon Lyonnaise des Eaux when the company was chosen by the European Space Agency to study the recycling of water during the future flights of space shuttle Hermes.[55] These and other accomplishments overshadow any shortcomings the French suppliers might have in dealing with dirty water. As one water authority chairman observed, 'The quality of water is not as good in France as in Britain. The French companies are technically not as good as the British. But their PR is very good'.[56]

It seems to me that this is another area in which the British can learn from the French. If the occasionally luckless image projected by the British water industry — the worst aspects of which were epitomised by South West Wa-

ter, branded the authority 'with a hole in its bucket' after Camelford and
the restricted service of summer 1989[57] — is a misrepresentation of its identity, then the industry had better set about projecting that identity in a more
favourable manner. This *could* be done. Quality *does* matter to the British
suppliers. Wessex Water's recent quality drive has reaped enormous dividends. Wessex achieves the highest levels of compliance on effluent (greater
than 95 per cent) and drinking water quality (99.7 per cent) of any water
plc in England and Wales. In November 1989, the company's Customer
Services division was runner-up to the British Quality Award conferred by
the British Quality Association, winning a high commendation for 'their
achievement in utilising modern technology to provide an excellent quality of service to the customer for their commitment to high standards of
performance'. Previous winners of the award include such big names as
IBM, Sony and Ford. Wessex was one of six companies recognised in 1989,
alongside ICI, British Steel, Avon Cosmetics and 3M UK. What was special
in Wessex Water's case, however, was that this was the first time that a
service company had come anywhere near winning the award.[58] Yet Wessex was prevented by government from publicising its achievement in the
run-up to privatisation: no water authority was to be perceived as being
intrinsically better (or worse — and this was difficult in the case of South
West Water, with the millstone of Camelford hanging round its neck) than
any other.

The British water authorities have acted as 'good citizens' in Third World
countries. The hand-dug well programme of the industry's charity, WaterAid, has helped to bring clean water to millions of villagers in Ghana,
Kenya, Uganda, India, Nepal and Sierra Leone.[59] More than 700 self-help
projects — whereby communities are given vital access to the simple technology and equipment which allows them to construct water systems, stor-
age tanks, wells and pipelines — have been supported by the charity. The
water plcs have vowed to continue to give WaterAid their backing after
privatisation. Perhaps they should also consider according a higher profile
to such image-improving activities: the days for hiding one's light under a
bushel are long gone.

Summary of conclusions

The perceived threat to the environment was among the most emotive issues
in the great water sell-off. How appropriate was it for private companies to
be responsible for a product which is a key determinant of public health?
The infectious disease problems of the Victorian era may have all but van-
ished in Western Europe, but the modern age has created problems of its
own. Against a backcloth of new global threats to humanity, the European
Commission is cracking down on the quality of drinking water throughout

the Community. Will French ownership of British water enhance or impede British compliance with EC directives on water quality?

Quality is notoriously difficult to define; but how a product or service or company is *perceived* is fundamental. The author of this report does not believe that the French water companies are technically far superior to the British. The drinking water directive is an exceedingly complex and exacting one, and Britain is far from being alone in her struggle to comply. Improvement programmes, which the French involvement can neither hasten nor hinder, are now being implemented in the UK. Yet there is clearly a problem of *image* — behind the so-called 'dirty man' of Europe, there may well be a clean man trying to get out. Britain is not the 'fen of stagnant waters' she is presented as being: her records on river cleanliness and sewage connection, for instance, are among the best in Europe. Wessex is the first service company to win a prestigious British Quality Award for high standards of performance. The French have problems of their own; but, perhaps through their experience of competition and the private sector, they have learned to foster a quality image, internalised by the workforce. This is a further area in which the British can learn from the French in the transition from the public sector, where image and identity matter less, to the private sector, where they are crucial.

Ultimately, however, while French company know-how may be exportable, the benefit of a government which ensures a continuing long-term perspective, and which remains in the wings to correct the short-sightedness of individual firms and markets, is not.

Notes

1. Quality, individualism, luxury and convenience are expected to become increasingly important to European Community consumers, according to the Economist Intelligence Unit. See 'EC consumer spending likely to rise 50 per cent in five years', *Financial Times*, 10 August 1989, p. 2. Quality is Charles Handy's fourth 'clue' to the future of organisations in industrialised countries. See Handy, C., op. cit., pp. 402–6.

2. Water and sanitation problems are responsible for 80 per cent of all disease in the Third World, and the deaths of 9 million children annually. Statistics supplied by WaterAid.

3. Sixty thousand fish were also killed when the poison was flushed out into rivers and streams. See, for example, 'DPP postpones Camelford poison case until after water sale', *Observer*, 19 November 1989.

4. The reports and their conflicting conclusions are discussed in 'Studies reveal brain damage from Camelford water pollution', *Guardian*, 24 July 1990, p. 1.

5. Cited in 'Les châteaux d'eau de la reine Victoria', *Le Monde*, 23 September 1989, pp. 27, 29.

6. There have been 14 cases directly attributable to nitrate in drinking water in the UK in the last 35 years, the last of which occurred in 1972. Friends of the Earth suggest, however, that the figure for the UK may be under-reported, because methaemoglobinaemia is not a notifiable disease and because the procedure to alert doctors to elevated nitrate levels has not always been observed. See HL Select Committee on the European Communities (1989), *Nitrate in Water*, op. cit., p. 10.

7. This was hypothesised by Sir Donald Acheson, the government's Chief Medical Officer, who in 1988 was asked to give an opinion on the health risks of nitrate. See Rose, C., op. cit., p. 80.

8. See 'Some British fish unsafe to eat, ministers admit', *Independent on Sunday*, 19 May 1991.

9. See 'Your tap water pure or poisoned', *Observer Magazine*, 6 August 1989.

10. The EC directive on drinking water quality defines maximum admissible concentrations of various pesticides without regard to their toxicity. Water suppliers must remove traces of apparently harmless pesticides as well as poisonous ones — at enormous cost. Department of the Environment officials therefore believe there is a strong case for reforming the directive in the area of pesticide control. But the key word here is apparently. It takes time for ill effects to emerge: should the reform go ahead, tomorrow's generation may not thank us for our lack of foresight. See 'Changes urged in water rules', *Independent*, 4 November 1988, p. 22.

11. Cited in Cook, J., op. cit., p. 9.

12. Greenpeace, *Against All Odds*, 1988.

13. Capra, F. (1982), *Turning Point: science, society and the rising culture*, Wildwood House, p. 3.

14. See 'Greenhouse catastrophe certain, say scientists', Observer, 19 August 1990.

15. Article 130R(2) of the Single European Act rules that 'environmental protection requirements shall be a component of the Community's other policies'.

16. Interestingly, Britain's Green Party ran an election campaign which focused specifically on sewage dumping at sea: 'To stop the flow of sewage, use your ballot paper'.

17. 'Cited in 'Leaders forced to heed the worried', The Times, 21 December 1989.

18. The view propounded by Friends of the Earth, and shared by West Germany's Grünen, is that modern industrial societies are 'inherently unsustainable'. See 'Mr Ridley and the politics of poetry', Financial Times, 10 March 1989, p. 15.

19. Crosby, P. B. (1979), Quality Is Free, McGraw-Hill, New York. IBM, Caterpillar and Michelin have adhered to this policy as a strategy for profitable market-share growth.

20. The level of service indicators specified by the DoE cover five services: water supply (connections, quantity, quality — where standards are related to EC directives); sewerage; environment; land drainage/flood protection; customer contact.

21. See 'Liquid liability', Financial Times, 8 May 1991, p. 16.

22. See 'Changes urged in water rules', op. cit.

23. Responsibility for lead in drinking water is held jointly by householder and supplier. While it is the duty of the latter to supply 'wholesome' water to the premises, provided that he has taken the necessary steps to reduce the plumbosolvency of water supplied through known lead pipes, it is up to the former to replace the pipes on his property. See Haigh, N., op. cit., p. 48.

24. Personal interview with the author, July 1989, Paris.

25. Personal interview with the author, June 1989.

26. Lyonnaise des Eaux Annual Report 1988, p. 9. Merchant writes that, for any organisational goal to succeed, internalisation by personnel at every tier of the organisation is vital. See Merchant, K., op. cit., p. 60.

27. Peters, T. J. and Waterman, R. H., op. cit., p. 181.

28. A state-by-state assessment of compliance with 1992 legislation is given in 'The good, the bad, and the indifferent', Financial Times, 25 September 1989, p. 20. This particular article claims that member states have failed to implement nine tenths of the EC directives which should by now be in force.

29. See Butt Philip, A. (1991), 'Westminster versus Brussels — the last crusade?', in Maclean, M. and Howorth, J., Europeans on Europe: transnational visions of a new continent, Macmillan, London, 1991, p. 196.

30. See Journal Officiel de la République Française: lois et décrets, 4 January 1989, pp.125–31.

31. The recent disclosure of the areas affected with high nitrate concentration, which included parts of South Staffordshire, is perhaps the key to why Générale des Eaux then sold part of its holding in the South Staffordshire water company.

32. Personal interview with the author, June 1989.

33. Personal interview with the author, June 1989.
34. See 'Britain on course for court battle on water standards', *Independent*, 9 February 1989, p. 2.
35. Cited in 'EC to take UK to court over tap water standards', *Financial Times*, 21 September 1989, p. 1.
36. See 'Britain in hot water with Commission', *Financial Times*, 8 February 1989, p. 2. Under the relevant article of the Treaty of Rome, the Commission sends a formal notice letter to the offending state, follows this up with a 'reasoned opinion' which clarifies the Commission's interpretation of EC law, and only goes to the European Court of Justice as a last resort.
37. See the *Fifth Annual Report to the European Parliament on Commission monitoring of the application of Community law* (1987), COM (88) 425, 3 October 1988. See also Siedentopf, H. and Ziller, J., eds. (1988), *Making European Policies Work: the implementation of Community legislation in Member States*, SAGE Publications, London. While this comparative study does not include a discussion of the drinking water directive itself, it does consider the implementation of directive 78/659/EEC on water standards for freshwater fish.
38. *Fifth Annual Report to the European Parliament on Commission monitoring of the application of Community law* (1987), op. cit., p. 40.
39. See, for example, 'Water authorities confused by row over quality', *Independent*, 11 February 1989, p. 3.
40. Quoted in 'EC to take UK to court over tap water standards', op. cit.
41. See 'Water sell-off falls foul of sewage crisis', *Observer*, 14 May 1989.
42. Cited in Rose, C., op. cit., p. 49.
43. See 'Minister hits back over report on declining river water quality', *Financial Times*, 1 March 1989, p. 13.
44. According to the National Water Council four-class system for grading rivers. Classes 1A and 1B support trout and/or salmon, and provide quality drinking water. Class 2 can support 'course' fish, but is used for drinking water only after advanced treatment. Class 3 contains no (or almost no) fish, while class 4 is heavily polluted. See Rose, C., op. cit., p. 55.
45. The 4,141 incidents of farm pollution in 1988 represented a rise of 6 per cent from 1987; yet during the same period prosecutions fell by 34 per cent, from 225 to 148. See ADAS/MAFF (1989), *Water Pollution from farm waste 1988 (England and Wales)*, Water Authorities Association Publications.
46. See, for example, 'Chief inspector for toxic waste and water quits', *Financial Times*, 19 November 1988, p. 4.
47. Details of the letter are given in 'Water chairmen attack sell-off "misinformation"', *Financial Times*, 18 March 1989, p. 6.
48. Mentioned in a personal interview, July 1989, Paris.
49. See 'Nous rebaignerons-nous un jour dans la Seine?', *Ça m'intéresse*, no. 35, January 1984, pp. 26–33.
50. Statistics given in the French daily *Libération*, 24 February 1988.

51. ibid.
52. See 'EC experts to discuss ban on sewage discharge in sea', *Financial Times*, 14 February 1989, p. 2.
53. See Institut pour une Politique Européenne de l'Environnement/Fondation Européenne de la Culture (1985), *Impact des directives eau et déchets en Allemagne Fédérale, France et Pays-Bas*, Paris. Volume II by Thierry Lavoux deals with France.
54. 'Si le temps continue à être défavorable, il faudra que la solidarité nationale joue son rôle', *Le Monde*, 13–14 May 1990, and 'Dix ans pour gagner la bataille de l'eau', *Le Monde*, 15–16 July 1991, p. 12.
55. See Lyonnaise des Eaux Annual Report 1988, p. 14.
56. Personal interview with the author, June 1989.
57. See, for example, 'Selling the board with a hole in its bucket', *Financial Times*, 20 September 1989, p. 10.
58. Personal interview with the author.
59. See the WaterAid journal *Oasis*, Spring 1989.

7 The British Water Industry in the 1990s: problems and prospects

We are part of the community of Europe, and we must do our duty as such — (Gladstone).

Organisations are living organisms, subject to daily — if often imperceptible — change. Since 1974, however, when the first oil crisis began to bite, we have lived in a turbulent world economy, where business life is characterised by its unpredictability; where external shocks with their often far-reaching effects (witness the repercussions on Western economies of the Gulf War) are commonplace; and where change, when it comes, is often rapid, violent and unforeseen.

So, in considering the future prospects of Britain's water businesses, the same proviso that is used to introduce and to qualify Paul Kennedy's discussion of future trends in his bestseller, *The Rise and Fall of the Great Powers* (1988), provides an appropriate beginning to this concluding chapter:

> Even the very recent past is history, and although problems of bias and source make the historian of the previous decade 'hard put to separate the ephemeral from the fundamental', he is still operating within the same academic discipline. But the writings upon how the present may evolve into the future, even if they discuss trends which are already under way, can lay no claim to being historical truth. Not only do the raw materials change, from archivally-based monographs to economic forecasts and political projections, but the validity of what is being written about can no longer be assumed. Even if there always were many methodological difficulties in dealing with 'historical facts', past events did indeed occur. Nothing one can say about the future has that certainty.[1]

With that caveat, this conclusion seeks to highlight those issues which may play a key role in determining the future prosperity, survival or demise of Britain's water businesses, and the obstacles which may prevent them from taking full advantage of the opportunities open to them, when, with the advent of the single market in 1993, competition in Europe becomes fiercer than ever before. It considers, in short, those 'differences which [may] make a difference' (Bateson, 1972) in the decade ahead. The chapter then comments on the likely evolution of the French stake in British water in the coming years, and considers how the French experiment may recur — rather, *how it is already recurring* — in other similarly low-risk, low-profile industries, traditionally perceived as unglamorous.

Finally, this conclusion seeks to elicit some of the broader implications of this episode for Britain and France in post-1992 Europe. And while I have no illusion about the rapidity with which the ideas, opinions and analyses presented in this book may be overtaken by the pace of change, it is nevertheless my hope that the picture presented in its pages will stand as a valid interpretation of the way in which Britain's water businesses faced up to a new environment and to new givens as they experienced at first hand, and in advance of the deadline, the realities of 1992.

'Differences which make a difference': determinants of future success

For most of the twentieth century, change in the British water industry was a protracted and relatively painless process: a slow but steady evolution stretching out over more than a hundred years, punctuated by various milestone Acts of Parliament. The British public took water largely for granted, an attitude encapsulated in one journalist's pertinent remark: 'flush and forget'. Water charges were modest — perhaps one explanation for the public's singular lack of interest in what is after all a vital industry, and for their similar lack of concern for its performance. Few people stopped to wonder whether the administrators who ran the authorities were actually doing a good job.

In the late 1980s, however, water came under the spotlight for the first time, as the pace of change quickened. With privatisation, a French invasion of the market by the backdoor through the Lilliputian world of the private water companies, a new focus on environmental standards throughout the European Community, and the sudden escalation of water charges, Britain's essentially public-sector water industry was thrown into a state of upheaval from which it is still reeling.

Controversial from the start, water privatisation proved to be more of a success than anyone had anticipated. With the public offer more than four times over-subscribed, it was against all expectations the second most popular privatisation of all time. The low share price was largely responsible; as Bryan Gould, Labour's shadow environment secretary put it, if one is offered ten pounds for a fiver, one does not say no. But perhaps all that the success of the flotation demonstrated was that any privatisation, however unpopular, however 'immoral' — the government did not actually own the assets it took it upon itself to sell (see above, Chapter 4) — can be made to succeed provided the price is right. The sell-off also benefitted from a clever promotional campaign, whose slogan, 'You too can be an H₂Owner', was almost as successful as the British Gas campaign to 'Tell Sid'. What was on sale, moreover, was not some giant national organisation, distant and anonymous; these were *local concerns*, with which the public could identify. The French water suppliers also played their part in the flotation's success. With so few shares allocated to Europe (only 3.6 per cent of the issue compared to 7.3 per cent for Japan alone)², the French preferred to wait until the first day of trading (12 December 1989) before bidding for shares, causing the share price to escalate in a flurry of activity.³

But if privatisation is now complete, *the far more important chapter of coming to terms with life in the private sector is still being written*. In effecting the crucial transition from public to private sector, many of the critical changes have still to be made. How individual water businesses fare in the task of adapting themselves to their new structures and to a new competitive environment in the short time available will go a long way towards determining their respective performances into the twenty-first century. The water businesses ought to aim to complete the process before the trade barriers go down in Europe, and certainly before the government waives its protective five-year 'golden share'. But what faith can there be now in golden shares, after the somewhat cavalier removal of the government's stake in Jaguar in the autumn of 1989? — the prelude to a takeover battle in which Ford and General Motors fought over the spoils, with Ford eventually winning the day. The offhand attitude displayed by Trade and Industry Secretary, Nicholas Ridley, at the time must inspire little confidence in those organisations which depend on golden shares for their protection from predators.

In considering the future success of Britain's water businesses, it is the contention of this report that much is likely to hinge on the answers to the following questions, discussed sequentially below:

1. Will management be allowed sufficient *room to manoeuvre*, given the tight regulation of the industry?
2. Will management teams have the necessary *ambition and capabilities*, given their public sector pasts?
3. Will the *culture change* from public to private sector be successfully effected at all tiers of the organisations concerned?
4. Will the water plcs be able to cultivate and project a favourable *image* in accordance with a new *identity* which assumes a genuine concern for the quality of product, service and the environment?

The need for a free hand

To date, tight government regulation has played a crucial role in prescribing the limits within which the management of water authorities and statutory companies alike have been free to act. As the industry emerges from the turmoil of the 1980s, how much will this really have changed?

The nature of competition in the water industry is such that the consumer must be protected from monopoly abuse. Management teams may come and go, ownership may change, and a certain amount of rationalisation may occur. (Ultimately the Three Valleys merger was allowed to proceed despite the 'sacrosanct' principle of comparative efficiency.) But nothing can prevent the company which survives these trials from operating an effective monopoly in its own area. The privatisation of companies which belong naturally in the private sector is one thing. There it can legitimately be claimed that privatisation exposes the companies concerned to the 'full commercial discipline of the customer'.[4] But as the OECD has stressed (see above, Chapter 3), it is quite another matter to privatise a public service in which competition makes little sense — the unnecessary duplication of distribution services would greatly increase costs if more than one supplier were to serve the same area — and where the customer is deprived of any choice but that of accepting the service he gets and paying the price demanded (Corfield, 1988). The threat of economic exploitation became all the more real in 1991 when, one by one, the privatised water and electricity plcs began to declare record profits despite a year of recession. A powerful regulatory regime was therefore vital; but the other side of the regulatory coin is the curtailment of managerial autonomy. Now, for the private water companies, profit control has given way to price control, while, for the privatised water authorities, what was effectively self-regulation has ceded to regulation by an array of external bodies. Britain's water businesses are to be monitored financially and environmentally, and it would be understandable if the combined constraints of a 6,000-strong National Rivers Authority, a 100-strong Office of Water Services headed by a potentially powerful Director General of Water, a new Drinking Water Inspectorate, a revamped Inspectorate of Pollution, a vigilant Monopolies and Mergers Commission, various local and regional Customer Services Committees, and an ever more exacting European Commission furnished with the information it needs by a newly created European Environmental Agency,[5] were to prove — quite simply — paralysing.

It is clear that the K factors issued by the Director General of Water will set company balance sheets for years to come.

To meet exacting EC drinking water standards to the letter, moreover, may prove to be a practical impossibility; but under British law the supply of sub-standard water is now a criminal offence, punishable by imprisonment.

Meanwhile, Brussels is making ready to cast its regulatory net even wider. A wastewater directive banning the dumping of sewage sludge at sea and enforcing higher standards of sewage treatment prior to its disposal through pipeline, is imminent, and the UK's highly expensive long sea-outfall programme seems set to come under attack. A further directive which aims to reduce phosphate in water is also planned. Already, there are more EC directives pertaining to aspects of water quality than to any other environmental issue.

Perhaps water plcs will attempt to expand through the takeover of private water companies in their area; but the proposed takeover of any water company with assets of more than £30 million is scrutinised by the MMC. The proposed merger of three water companies in the South East was eventually allowed to proceed. But not until the MMC and DTI had provocatively kept their French parent companies waiting for a year, causing their interest to cool,[6] as the plan was deliberated and, at one stage, rejected despite the significant cost savings — and hence reduced bills — it was bound to mean for customers in the area.

No doubt Britain's larger water businesses will try to acquire other companies in their region which operate in related areas, as they struggle to diversify. However, Severn Trent's £78 million hostile bid for the Caird waste disposal group ended in failure.

Last but by no means least, management teams with limited experience of the private sector are themselves already being threatened by the 'stick' of the capital market. A fortnight after privatisation, the management of Anglian Water was having to come to terms with the fact that Lyonnaise des Eaux had already acquired a 9 per cent stake in the company.

Under Margaret Thatcher, privatisation was a political end in itself. Widening share ownership was believed to help swell the ranks of Conservative voters, and her re-election for a second and then a third term has sometimes been attributed to the fact that she sold off council houses and privatised British Telecom and British Gas (see above, Chapter 3). Mrs Thatcher, however, is no longer in Downing Street, and some of the government's policies may have changed as a result. Most notably, Cabinet government has been restored; hostility to European integration is now couched in more conciliatory tones, even if the fundamental message remains constant;[7] the poll tax has been recognised as the electoral liability that it was, and key amendments made to it; and a more favourable attitude to state investment seems to have been adopted, as evinced by the last-minute reprieve of the Channel tunnel rail-link project, once axed by the Iron Lady for want of private funds and government foresight.

But some things, however, have *not* changed, and amongst these is privatisation. The new man at no. 10 has already affirmed that for as long as he continues at the helm, there is to be no slackening of pace. However, if the enormous upheaval to companies and industries and the huge cost of restructuring are to have any economic justification, privatisation ought to be first and foremost a *means* to improving industry performance and customer service. Ultimately, one cannot avoid the question: *are privatised organisations necessarily superior to public ones?* Is a privatised monopoly potentially any less harmful than one which is state-owned? The record profits announced by electricity and water plcs in 1991 suggest not. On the other hand, what will have been achieved if the water plcs are to be constantly looking over their shoulder? If controls are so tight that they have no 'rope', no room to perform, to innovate and experiment, to reap some of the benefits of this costly move to the private sector? Even more strongly regulated than they were in the public sector, there is a danger that the water plcs may fall between two stools. That in relation to their more dynamic, entrepreneurial and autonomous competitors — the French suppliers, which operate an effective oligopoly at home, and which the French themselves describe as difficult to control — they may remain forever hybrids, private-sector eunuchs, burdened with regulation and hence unable to shake off their public-sector legacies.

If the managers of the water services plcs are to be denied freedom of action in their core business, they may be forced to make their profits elsewhere. Only non-core subsidiaries escape the confines of government regulation — which bodes ill for environmental protection (land development is already underway in the South West, where Wessex Water has launched a joint venture with Wimpey). Success here is likely to be conditional upon the existence of synergies between core and non-core businesses (Ansoff, 1965; Ecole des Mines, 1989), upon management quality and ambition (Ansoff, 1965), and on the ability of management to raise the necessary funds, in the form of debt or equity, with which to finance their proposals — so managerial autonomy depends in turn on business confidence.

But the collective mechanisms whereby business confidence is constructed and buoyed up are fragile (Berger, 1987). And while low-risk water shares might seem attractive as a relatively stable element in an investment portfolio (Markowitz, 1959),[8] with water shares outperforming the market by an average of 34 per cent in 1990 as the recession set in, the political risk associated with them ought not to be underestimated.[9] Opposition threats to renationalise the industry in the event of a Labour election victory are not likely to encourage private investment in the long term.[10] Labour party discourse has replaced the term 'renationalisation' with 'social ownership', a fate reserved only for the large public services such as water and gas, the change in terminology reflecting that society as a whole rather than the state would be the main beneficiary. Yet even if Labour did not go so far as to renationalise, the mere appointment of a hostile Director General of Water could potentially wreck the finances of the water plcs.[11] Lord Crickhowell, formidable head of the NRA, is known to be keen to impose even higher standards of sewage treatment than are currently being debated for the EC's new wastewater directive—but at a cost of up to £15 billion to the companies. The companies, however, are currently protected by a relatively 'water-plc-friendly' Director of Ofwat, concerned to keep increases to water bills within politically acceptable limits. Such protection may prove to be shortlived, should Labour win the coming election.

The regulatory regime itself is a further disincentive to invest: the recent under-performance of both British Gas and British Telecom on the Stock Exchange has been attributed to regulatory uncertainties. Moreover, having just sought to raise a total of £8 billion of working capital from international banks, in one of the largest fund-raising exercises from banks to be undertaken in sterling to date, the water plcs would be ill-advised to saddle themselves with further debt which they do not yet know that they can service.[12]

When the privatisation of the industry was first announced, water chiefs may have looked forward to having a free hand. It seems, however, that they are to be bound hand and foot. While it is right that the customer should be protected as far as possible, the government should be aware that the effect of confining the water plcs to regulatory strait-jackets may be to stifle the entrepreneurial life out of them. That the government does not seem unduly perturbed by this suggests that water privatisation was never intended as an *economic means* but only ever as a *political end*.

The need for management capability

Management quality is likely to be a key factor in determining both how management teams respond to this formidable regulatory regime, and how investors differentiate between the various water businesses. To thrive in adverse regulatory circumstances, to resist responding in kind to 'creeping bureaucracy' (this is what some say the National Rivers Authority threatens to become, and what some accuse the European Commission of being already) requires that 'entrepreneurial behaviour' come to the fore within the firm. Ansoff (1965) defines this as a concern for the strategic and an ability to manage the discontinuous. He opposes entrepreneurial behaviour to 'competitive behaviour', defined as a concern for the operational and incremental.[13] But even competitive behaviour presupposes competition, to which the British water industry has not in the past been accustomed. To what extent, then, can the former public-sector administrators of Britain's water businesses wake up and become entrepreneurial? New recruits can help here. Many of the water services plcs have already recruited new management from the private sector. To such an extent, indeed, that the *Financial Times* dubbed the privatisation of the water authorities as potentially 'the most extensive board restructuring in history'.[14]

Strategic capability on the part of management—the ability to achieve chosen objectives both in self-generated tasks and in handling major externally or internally generated issues—will be vital to success. ('If I get it wrong I shall be sacked—and rightly so', said one water authority chairman.[15]) Essentially, strategic capability is about meeting the challenges of the future. The challenges of the 1990s, as the French water suppliers have shown by their European growth strategy, are concerned with the need to venture abroad and gain global market share, perhaps through forming alliances with foreign competitors in order to have the necessary 'clout' or critical mass for survival and prosperity. Here, language proficiency and an understanding of other cultures will be paramount. Since 1988, the employees of one water authority have been undergoing intensive language training in French with a language consultancy consortium. It has also been investigating the German market, which seems, however, to be very much tied up. The challenges of the 1990s are also about gaining share in the virgin markets of the East, which is in urgent need of infrastructural repair and environmental rehabilitation. In 1990, Lyonnaise des Eaux again led the way, signing a contract with the German construction giant Thyssen for a joint venture in the former East Germany.

But the future is likely to be equally concerned with consolidating one's position at home, where national champions are no longer to be protected from foreign invaders, even in vital utilities like water, and even when the predator is a state-controlled company. It has been said that the reason why the British government did not, initially, object to French forays into British water was because the companies concerned were from the private sector. So there would be no 'nationalisation by the backdoor'. Yet government resistance to the takeover of private companies in the UK by state-controlled firms from abroad has not prevented a number from being cleared (including one joint venture between Elf Aquitaine, the French state-controlled oil group, and the US Engelhard Corporation to buy UK oil refining assets).[16] In the late 1980s France emerged, somewhat surprisingly perhaps, as the Community's principal cross-border acquirer. Many of these mergers and acquisitions were made by groups under state control. Many of their targets were of British provenance.

When the decision was taken by government to float all ten water authorities together, it became paramount that no authority should be perceived as being intrinsically better or worse than any other, lest investors flock to some to the detriment of others. Every effort was therefore made to iron out any disparities of management quality, of investment prospects, which might—and do—exist. The attempt at equalisation was difficult to sustain. In our small and overcrowded island, property is one of the most prized assets. Situated in the South East, still Britain's most prosperous region despite feeling the bite of the recession more keenly than the North, Thames Water has development prospects which vastly outstrip those of any other water plc, as Colin Chapman explains:

From Lechlade to Teddington, where the River Thames becomes tidal, there were locks, pumping stations, footpaths, gardens. Like British Rail's stations, these had huge development potential, not as office blocks, but as marinas and other centres of leisure serving the public. The same was true along the Thames' many tributaries. Then there was the river itself: popular in some key places, but generally under-utilized as a source of pleasure and as a means of transport.[17]

The management of South West Water, on the other hand, has had its credibility severely damaged by poisoned supplies, by the emotive sight of stand-pipes at street-corners throughout the drought of summer 1989, and by the dirty beaches of Torquay. Perusal of the *Water Bulletin* supplement which recorded 'who's who' in the new water plcs in the wake of privatisation revealed considerable staffing disparities between them. While some had 'quality managers', 'overseas managers', 'business development managers', 'business planning and marketing managers' (there was no marketing manager in any water authority prior to 1987, when one was recruited at Thames Water), these appointments were lacking in others. South West Water, for instance, had a 'customer services policy manager', a 'compliance and quality assurance manager' and a 'legal adviser'. In the light of Camelford, and the prosecution of the board of the former South West Water Authority,[18] it was not surprising that these posts were yet to be filled at the time.[19] Still, the company put its best foot forward. The cover of its 1990 Annual Report read 'Quality, Reliability, Growth'; but still doubts remained.

The need to make the necessary culture jump

There is an old Turkish proverb which observes that 'you can put a gold saddle on a donkey; but it is still a donkey'. Many of the water services plcs have recruited new management since privatisation, as mentioned above. But, old or new, management is effective *only where its capability is compatible with the prevalent organisational culture*. Compatibility matters because culture can impede or facilitate entrepreneurial behaviour within the firm in the following important ways:

— Culture can allow strategic issues to be appreciated and understood (or not).

— It can permit (or impede) drastic solutions, when these prove necessary.

— Its rituals can enhance (or inhibit) speed of response.

Whether a climate of receptivity to new issues can be fostered within Britain's water businesses will clearly be crucial to their future success. It is one thing for the small private water companies to seek to change their corporate cultures. Where these are owned by a French supplier, the French parent is almost bound to act as a powerful lever for change. But organisational change is more difficult when the company concerned is a large one and has a public sector legacy stretching back a long way. While one study of privatisation in the UK by Bishop and Kay (1988) found that privatisation has had beneficial effects in modifying the culture of British business in general, it also discovered that privatisation is not of itself sufficient to alter the character of individual companies.[20] Chapman notes that, if some privatised companies have seen little change of style, others have experienced nothing less than a 'cultural revolution'.[21] Charismatic leadership, where this exists or can be drafted in, can act as an effective change agent. The particular personality of the man at the top is seen as crucial in British organisations — much more so than in France, where it is the power of the position which confers authority rather than the charisma of the individual which commands it (Barsoux and Lawrence, 1990; Lane, 1989). Nevertheless, it is not enough for water chiefs alone to make the culture leap. Financially, they have much to gain from privatisation, which has proved highly profitable to the managers of companies privatised to date.[22] But for culture change to be more than simply cosmetic, *everyone in the organisation must make it*. To alter attitudes requires that staff at all levels be made to feel personally involved. British Airways is one example of a large public-sector enterprise which, at the time of its transition to the private sector, successfully altered attitudes throughout the organisation, achieved partly as a result of sending one third of all staff on a two-day course entitled 'Putting People First'.

The required culture jump is also likely to prove more difficult for the water plcs than for the private water companies because many more water authority workers may have opposed privatisation than either government or management cared to admit. There is a danger that conflicting cultures may arise which then seek to compete with one another. When the chairman of North West Water, Dennis Grove, announced that his staff were strongly in favour of privatisation, several employees were moved to write to the *Guardian* in protest, maintaining that water workers were like the remainder of the population: '70 per cent ... against the measure'. They claimed further to 'fear for their rights [after privatisation] and the difficulty of carrying out an essential service in an atmosphere of profit maximisation'.[23]

Clearly, the task of persuading a disaffected workforce at North West Water to make the necessary culture jump will be problematic. Wessex Water, however, has grasped the importance of employee participation in the success of culture change. Regular team briefings are held, in order to enhance employee understanding of the company's mission ('to provide our customers with a high quality, reliable, efficient water and sewerage service; to expand the range of our services both at home and overseas; to care for the environment and to create new opportunities for our employees') and 'quality first' ethos ('to fully involve all employees at all levels in the achievement of our mission; to keep everyone fully informed and to continually improve the quality of service to all customers both internal and external').[24]

The need for a favourable image

Finally, the British water industry as a whole needs to shake off its image as the 'dirty man' of Europe — especially since, industry chiefs allege, that image accords ill with the industry's true identity (see above, Chapter 6). With the Camelford poison case of 1988, a strong anti-privatisation sentiment throughout England and Wales, prosecution looming in the European Court of Justice, and consumers having to bear the brunt of higher charges for the foreseeable future, significant damage has been done to the industry through bad publicity. If individual water businesses wish to prosper in the 1990s, then it is vital that they project a *greener image* than at present — one which is above all concerned with *quality*: quality of life, of product, of service to the customer. The future of the water industry lies first and foremost in its becoming an environmental industry. This is vital if it is to restore and retain the confidence of the consumer; if it is to be regarded as a valued partner of government; and if it is to become a fully-fledged negotiating partner for the European Commission, with whom it will increasingly have to deal.

Why, one might ask, should water plcs and private companies be concerned about their image, now that privatisation has been successfully effected, and given that each will operate an effective monopoly in its own area? While image and identity matter less in the public sector, in the private sector they are crucial. Expansion possibilities are far greater in non-core activities where the company concerned may not have a monopoly than they are in the core business. Good relations with the local community will be vital to the success of profit-making non-core activities: everyone needs clean water, but not everyone needs, say, cable television. An improved image abroad will help international ventures succeed. How foreign customers are expected to have faith in the water purification consultancy recently set up by Yorkshire Water, which is responsible for two of the dirtiest rivers in Britain, is unclear.[25]

One of the ten water services plcs, however, has already made significant headway in achieving a quality image. The management of Wessex Water has grasped the importance of achieving total quality in every aspect of its business. The company seeks to represent this ethos with the logo 'Quality First', and at the time of privatisation, was the only one of the ten to have demonstrated its commitment to quality by appointing a Quality Manager.

What can the British expect from the French in the water business?

What can the British expect from the French in the water business in the coming months and years? The short answer to that question would seem to be 'more of the same'.

The French water suppliers are likely to continue to increase their share of the British water market. On 19 December 1989, Lyonnaise des Eaux declared its provisional hand, the only one of the trio to do so. In the short space of one week, shocking directors of the newly-privatised companies by the speed of their move, Lyonnaise des Eaux purchased holdings of 9 per cent, 6 per cent and 2 per cent in Anglian, Wessex and Severn-Trent respectively, amounting to an investment of £120 million after payment of the last two instalments.[26] One year later, however, in a sudden about-turn, Lyonnaise des Eaux-Dumez placed its stakes in Severn Trent and Wessex Water on the market, an action which doubtless pleased the management boards of the companies concerned. But the 9 per cent stake in Anglian water was retained; almost as if after a twelve-month trial run, hounds had finally decided which fox to pursue. This key stake is quite clearly an excellent base from which to launch a potential takeover bid following the lapse of the golden share ruling in 1994, perhaps bolstered by further share-chasing in the intervening period. However, Anglian would do well to regard the French involvement in a positive light. The densely fertilised soil of East Anglia has given rise to drinking water which is laced with nitrates. This is a problem which is particularly familiar to the French water companies: France is the most heavily farmed country of the Community. There is clearly much scope for technological collaboration in this domain.

Although Lyonnaise des Eaux-Dumez seems to have called a halt to additional market purchases in the meantime, this may prove to be little more than a temporary breathing-space: the group has claimed on previous occasions to have drunk its fill of British water.

In the medium to long term, we are likely to see Lyonnaise des Eaux-Dumez develop from being a French company with a European presence into a *European* company—a network of European companies—with a *global* presence. Already, the merger with Dumez has done much to realise the group's worldwide aspirations.

Générale des Eaux and SAUR are also thought to have built up stakes, albeit smaller ones, in Britain's water plcs. But unlike Lyonnaise, Générale's stakes will have been built up in full consultation with the boards of the companies concerned, while SAUR is expected to announce a joint venture with South West Water.

Rationalisation may also be on the agenda, both for the water companies and for the water services plcs. The positive outcome of the MMC investigation into the proposed merger of three private water companies (Lee Valley,

Colne Valley and Rickmansworth), to form 'Three Valleys Water Services' in which Générale des Eaux has a controlling interest, is likely to have important implications for the future shape of the industry. By this merger, the principle that the maximum number of comparators be retained has been breached. Small businesses in general are likely to have a tougher time in the coming decade than in the 1980s, as competition becomes fiercer than ever before, and clearly, the smaller water companies are bound to have to fight for their survival, if only because a certain amount of rationalisation makes sense. And while the government's notion of 'comparative competition' does give them a modicum of protection against the larger water plcs, nevertheless they remain vulnerable to attack by other parties, such as companies engaged in the supply of pipes or pumps, or the construction and design of treatment plants. The merging of water companies contiguous to one another is one way in which they might seek to avoid being swallowed up by predators.

Although some rationalisation is certainly on the cards for the water plcs after 1994 (Northumbrian, the smallest, nine times oversubscribed at the time of its flotation, and South West Water, with the poorest image of the ten water services plcs, are perhaps the likeliest candidates for takeover), full-scale rationalisation is not. This is largely because there is an optimal size for water distribution and — particularly — sewage disposal (see above, Chapter 3). That optimal size coincides more or less with the existing river basins. As the arena for political decision-making within the European Community shifts from national seats of government to Brussels, and assumes a federal and more decentralised structure, the region, and with it the local community, is likely to come into its own, helping to create a favourable climate within which the water services plcs can operate.

What can the British expect from the French in other businesses?

If a single theme has dominated the French penetration of the UK water market during 1988 and 1989, it was that it evinced the growing realisation on the part of the French that '1992' was soon to become a reality, and that significant market share must be gained in advance. During 1989, European merger and acquisition activity reached fever pitch. But it was France and the US which jockeyed for position as the major cross-border acquirers in Europe: in the first six months of the year, the value of deals undertaken by French companies totalled Ecu 4.1 billion, with the US in second place (Ecu 3.61 billion) and Britain coming third (Ecu 3.26 billion).[27] In all this activity, the DTI single market slogan 'open for business' took on fresh significance, with the UK emerging as the major target of cross-border bids: 18 per cent of all European takeovers involved a British prey. In the case of acquisitions by French companies, it might be said that insult was added to injury, for in many cases the British were prevented from retaliating due to the in-built protection afforded by crossed shareholdings and *autocontrôle*.[28] So the episode which we have studied here is far from being an isolated incident. Many of the British businesses which have attracted French interest are similarly low-risk, low-profile service industries: waste collection, street cleaning, heating, health care, funeral services. With the growing tendency for national governments — not only in the UK — to contract out essential municipal services, these businesses offer significant prospects for expansion. They are also attractive because, like water, they are extremely low-risk, being largely unaffected by the vagaries of national economies: everybody needs health care, everybody eventually dies. In the words of one water company general manager, '[the French] are literally trying to look after their customers from the cradle to the grave'.[29] And we all, in our lives, produce mountains or rubbish which must be cleared away. Already, the French have made considerable inroads into Britain's £260 million rubbish-collection and street-cleaning market. In June 1991, a beleaguered Liverpool council voted to award the rubbish-collection contract of its refuse-ridden city to Onyx (owned by Générale de Eaux), when the company offered to do the job for half the fee charged by the councils own dustmen. Already, Onyx has won over twenty contracts to clean up Britain's streets, while Sitaclean Technology, part-owned by Lyonnaise des Eaux-Dumez, has won ten.

Privatisation in the UK has opened doors to the French. The CGE subsidiary Associated Gas Services (AGS) has managed to enter the British gas market by offering industrial customers cheaper supplies than they can obtain from British Gas — quite an achievement given the 98 per cent share of the industrial gas market currently enjoyed by British Gas. James McKinnon, head of Ofgas, hopes to reduce that stake to a healthier 90 per cent in the near future;[30] no doubt AGS will seek to exploit this greater bias towards competition. Its sister company, Associated Heat Services also stands to benefit from the privatisation of electricity: cheap nuclear power from France should enable the company to undercut the price of British-produced electricity.[31]

This book has been about the French investment in British water. And yet, even as I write the conclusion, that investment has been dwarfed by others. In its Annual Report for 1988, Générale des Eaux announced that it had taken steps towards the purchase of British hospitals.[32] In the spring of 1990, the group made public the purchase of AMI Healthcare, Britain's leading chain of private clinics, through its subsidiary Générale de Santé. At an overall cost of £245 million for the chain, which comprised 18 clinics and 1,400 beds, this was three times the amount the group had invested in British water (£80 million).[33] Within a year, the number of private clinics owned by the group in the UK had risen to 21, representing a total of 1,540 beds.[34] With government moves afoot to partially privatise the National Health Service, the company's stake building is unlikely to stop there.

Meanwhile in the summer of 1989 France's largest undertaker, Pompes Funèbres Générales, arranged a merger between two of Britain's three publicly quoted funeral directors, Hodgson Holdings and Kenyon Securities, from which it emerged with around 25 per cent of the combined business. The group's philosophy is identical to that of the water suppliers: to expand both geographically and in ancillary areas.[35] Lyonnaise des Eaux-Dumez is one of the company's major shareholders. In 1991 the third of Britain's one-time big three was targeted. In capturing a substantial stake in PKHI, the French consolidated their position in the British funeral market, and renewed their assault on the British way of death: continental burial practices are expected to follow, accompanied by yet more EC legislation.

Conclusion

After privatisation, three of the seven largest water companies in the world became British. In the cut-and-thrust of the private sector, following the lapse of the government's golden shares only Thames Water and Welsh Water will be protected from predatory advances: the former because of its size, and the latter because of a special ruling obtained by the Welsh Secretary.

It is the contention of this book that the government's golden share ruling may have given some of the water plcs a chance to escape the fate suffered by their smaller brethren, the private water companies. The 15 per cent ceiling on foreign holdings has left them free to form partnerships of their own choosing. The ball is to some extent in their court. Alliances — which the French companies are actively seeking with newly privatised authorities — are clearly preferable to acquisitions. Partnerships are reciprocal arrangements where two parties collaborate for mutual benefit from a position of comparative equality, and jointly reap the fruits of their efforts; but takeover implies the surrender of overall control.

The days of national champions — often too small for global competition, yet too large to be supported by domestic markets alone (Berger, 1987) — are definitively over. And if European firms are to compete effectively at international level, we need to find some means whereby some of Europe's minnows can grow into bigger fish, even at the expense of others going to the wall (Sharp and Shearman, 1987).[36] Collaboration between European firms can help us overcome the problems caused by our former compartmentalisation. There are many areas in which collaboration might prove possible in the water industry, and research and development — in order that a larger combined sum of money might be better spent on improving the quality of our water, without the repetition of projects on both sides of the Channel—is a particularly obvious one. To this end, Générale des Eaux has already set up a Franco-British research club.

The British water industry has come a long way from those days in the early 1980s when, as it was busy administering itself, the French water companies first took a look at the UK water market. Then the British suppliers were barely at stage one in Simon's schema for the solution of any decision problem—the stage of perception of need or opportunity (see above, Chapter 1). Now they have reached stage three: the evaluation of alternatives for their respective contributions. In the words of one water chief: 'It is not all going to happen. And anything is being considered'. As the water businesses move on to stage four—the choice of one or more alternatives for implementation—let us hope that among their aspirations is also that of being among the world's best as well as the world's biggest. Room to manoeuvre, management quality and ambition, compatibility of culture and capability, and a quality image to match a genuine quality identity, characterised by concern for the environment and customer alike, are all vital ingredients to success. Fruitful collaboration with the French may enhance it.

Notes

1. Kennedy, P. (1989), *The Rise and Fall of the Great Powers*, Fontana Press, London, p. 565.

2. In addition, institutional investors in Canada and the US were accorded 1.6 per cent and 1.3 per cent of the issue respectively. See 'Buoyant debut for water likely as institutions chase shares', *Financial Times*, 12 December 1989, p. 1.

3. On the first day of trading, the uniform partly-paid share price of 100p rose to between 139p (for Severn-Trent) and 157p (for Northumbrian).

4. 1987 Conservative Election Manifesto.

5. It was agreed in late 1989 to set up a European Environmental Agency (interestingly, the British were initially opposed to the idea), to be responsible for the collection and publication of information on such issues as water quality, pollution and the health of flora and fauna.

6. An article in the French daily, *Le Monde*, cites this prolonged prevarication on the part of the Trade and Industry Secretary as the main reason behind a certain loss of enthusiasm for British water on the part of the French trio. See 'La Bourse de Londres trouve l'eau trop tiède', *Le Monde*, 15–16 April 1990.

7. Consider, for example, the stance adopted by Chancellor Norman Lamont over the proposed single currency. In May 1991, at a conference on economic and monetary union organised by the Royal Institute of International Affairs and the Association for the Monetary Union of Europe, Norman Lamont made it clear that Britain's position on EMU had not changed, despite her concern that member states should move forward together. See, for example, 'Chancellor stands firm over single currency', *Financial Times*, 31 May 1991, pp. 1, 14.

8. Markowitz's portfolio perspective of investment theory recognised that the risk of any individual investment must be evaluated in the context of the whole. See Markowitz, H. M. (1959), *Portfolio Selection: efficient diversification of investment*, John Wiley and Jones, New York.

9. UBS Phillips and Drew, op. cit., p. 90.

10. All of the opposition parties were opposed to the flotation. Both Labour and the Green Party are committed to returning the industry to the public sector. The Social and Liberal Democrats would not hesitate to do so 'if it becomes clear that [this is] the only way to achieve ... vital objectives' (specified as quality standards, accountability to consumers, etc.). The Social Democratic Party has vowed to judge the privatised water businesses on their merits, and to review their ownership if necessary. See 'The political risk: party lines on water', *Financial Times*, Supplement on the Water Sale, 25 November 1989, p. XI. Of the above, only the Labour Party represents a serious contender to the present government in the immediate future. Labour would do well to reflect that, however convincing the argument for 'social ownership' of water, the cultural and financial damage to the water plcs of having to readjust to the public sector would be considerable. It was partly for this reason that, when the French Socialist Party was returned to power in the legislative elections of June 1988, there was no renationalisation of privatised companies.

11. He could do so by not allowing items of expenditure to be eligible for 'cost pass-through'; by underestimating the costs of meeting new obligations; or by dramatically reducing K factors after the five-year review period. See UBS Phillips and Drew, op. cit., p. 83.

12. See 'Working capital of £8bn sought by water authorities', *Financial Times*, 21 August 1989, p. 16.

13. Ansoff, I., op. cit., pp. 197-8.

14. Cited in 'Privatised water boards take on fresh crews', *Financial Times*, 2 September 1989, p. 4.

15. Reported in 'Wessex 90', *Wessex News*, no. 9, November 1989, p. 2.

16. See 'Lilley clears three acquisitions by foreign groups', *Financial Times*, 31 May 1991, p. 7.

17. Chapman, C., op. cit., p. 46.

18. The prosecution was brought against the water authority residuary body, a 'ghost' organisation which remains in the public sector, the government having decided that the company could not be sold as a whole while under threat of a substantial fine.

19. See 'Who's Who in the water plcs', *Water Bulletin*, Supplement, 1 September 1989.

20. Reported in 'Privatisation as an end in itself', op. cit.

21. Chapman, C., op. cit., p. 105.

22. In 1979, the top executives of British Airways and British Gas earned £45,000 and £49,000; in 1988, their salaries had increased by a factor of six and four respectively, to £253,000 and £184,000. See Bishop and Kay, op. cit.

23. Cited in 'Straining the water workers' facts', *Guardian*, 14 August 1989, p. 18.

24. See *A Briefer's Guide to Team Briefing*, Wessex Water.

25. See 'Polluters to turn water purifiers', *Independent*, 25 May 1989.

26. See 'Swimming for beginners while the sharks circle', *Financial Times*, 19 December 1989, p. 23.

27. Given in 'France and US set the pace', *Financial Times*, Supplement on Top 500 1989, 19 December 1989, p. IV.

28. While the French Senate voted in 1989 to prevent companies from defending themselves against takeover through *autocontrôle*, it will be some considerable time before existing crossed shareholdings are undone. See 'France votes to stamp out takeover defence ploy', *Financial Times*, 13 June 1989, p. 30.

29. Personal interview with the author, June 1989.

30. See 'Ofgas presses for more competition', op. cit.

31. See 'Company seeks cheap French power deal', op. cit.

32. Reported in Compagnie Générale des Eaux Annual Report 1988, p. 11.

33. See 'La Générale des eaux en Grande Bretagne', *Le Monde*, 10 March 1990, p. 29.

34. Reported in 'Cliniques privées: adieu, beaux rêves', *L'Expansion*, 7–20 February 1991, p. 56.

35. See 'French target UK undertakers', *Independent*, 19 July 1989, p. 13.

36. Many of those that fail may be British. Poor profit showings are frequently a prelude to takeover, and thirteen of the twenty-five European companies suffering the largest profit decreases in 1989 were British. See 'France and US set the pace', op. cit.

Bibliography

The following lists include only that material which has proved useful in the preparation of this study.

Primary sources

Company statements

Annual Reports for 1987, 1988 and 1989 for the following companies: Anglian Water; Northumbrian Water; North West Water; Severn Trent; Southern Water; South West Water; Thames Water; Welsh Water; Wessex Water; Yorkshire Water; Bristol Waterworks; Essex Water; Mid-Sussex Water; North Surrey Water; West Kent Water; Compagnie Générale des Eaux; Société Lyonnaise des Eaux (now renamed Lyonnaise des Eaux-Dumez).

Bristol Waterworks, *Letter to Shareholders*.

Wessex Water, *A Briefer's Guide to Team Briefing*.

Wessex Water, *Wessex News*.

Interviews with managers and directors of water businesses in Britain and France.

Official publications

Commission of the European Communities (1987), *Europe Without Frontiers: completing the internal market*.

Conservative Election Manifesto, 1987.

Consumers in the European Community Group (1987), *The Quality of Drinking Water: a consumer view*, CECG, London.

Countryside Commission (1988), *Water: the case for the countryside.*

Department of Trade and Industry, *Europe open for Business.*

Department of Trade and Industry, *Single Market News.*

European Commission, *Eurobarometer.*

European Movement, *Facts.*

Fifth Annual Report to the European Parliament on Commission monitoring of Community law (1987), COM (88) 425, 3 October 1988.

Greenpeace (1988), *Against All Odds.*

House of Lords Select Committee on the European Communities (1989), *Nitrate in Water*, HL Paper 73.

Institut National de la Statistique et des Etudes Economiques, *Tableaux de l'Economie Française* (annually).

Institut pour une Politique Européenne de l'Environnement/Fondation Européenne de la Culture (1985), *Impact des directives eau et déchets en Allemagne Fédérale, France et Pays-Bas*, Paris.

Journal Officiel de la République Française: lois et décrets.

Monopolies and Mergers Commission (1990), *Report on the Merger of General Utilities plc and the Mid Kent Water Company*, Cmnd. 1125.

Monopolies and Mergers Commission (1990), *Report on the Merger of Southern Water and the Mid Sussex Water Company*, Cmnd. 1126.

NALGO (1988), *Report on NALGO's delegation to the French water industry.*

Price Waterhouse (1987), *Privatisation: the facts.*

Report of the UK Water Industry Trade Unions' Delegation to the CGT in Paris on 28th/29th September 1988.

Syndicat Professionnel des Distributeurs d'Eau (1980), *Le Livre bleu de l'eau potable.*

UBS Phillips and Drew (1989), *The Water Industry in England and Wales.*

Water Authorities Association, Ministry of Agriculture, Fisheries and Food (1989), *Water Pollution and Farm Waste 1988: England and Wales.*

Water Companies Association (1990), *Water Supply Companies Factbook.*

Water Bulletin, the journal of the water industry.

White Paper on 'the Privatisation of the Water Authorities in England and Wales', Cmnd. 9734.

WaterAid, *Oasis (the journal of the water industry's charity).*

Secondary sources

Books and monographs

Ansoff, I. (1965), *Corporate Strategy*, Penguin Books, Harmondsworth.

Ascher, K. (1987), *The Politics of Privatisation: contracting out public services*, Macmillan, London.

Balladur, E. (1987), *Je crois en l'Homme plus qu'en l'Etat*, Flammarion, Paris.

Balladur, E. (1989), *Passion et longueur de temps*, Fayard, Paris.

Barsoux, J.-L. and Lawrence, P. (1990), *Management in France*, Cassell, London.

Bayliss, B. T. and Butt Philip, A. A. S. (1980), *Capital Markets and Industrial Investment in Germany and France*, Saxon House, Farnborough.

Birch, T. (1989), *Poison in the System*, Greenpeace, London.

Bizaguet, A. (1988), *Le Secteur Public et les privatisations*, Presses Universitaires de France, Paris.

Bishop, M. and Kay, J. (1988), *Does Privatisation Work? Lessons from the UK*, London Business School, London.

Cawson, A. et al. (1990), *Hostile Brothers: competition and closure in the European electronics industry*, Clarendon Press, Oxford.

Cecchini, P. (1988), *The European Challenge: 1992 — the benefits of a Single Market*, Gower, London.

Chapman, C. (1990), *Selling the Family Silver: has privatization worked?*, Hutchinson Business Books, London.

Clutterbuck, D. and Goldsmith, W. (1984), *The Winning Streak*, Weidenfeld and Nicholson, London.

Cook, J. (1989), *Dirty Water*, Unwin, London.

Corfield, The Rt. Hon. Sir F. V. (1988), *Water Privatisation and the Consumer*, Selsdon Group, Stroud.

Crampton, S. (1990), *1992: Eurospeak Explained*, Rosters Ltd, in association with Consumers in the European Community Group, London.

Crosby, P. B. (1979), *Quality is Free*, McGraw-Hill, New York.

Cyert, R. M. and March, J. G. (1963), *Behavioural Theory of the Firm*, Prentice Hall International, Hemel Hempstead.

De Belot, J. (1987), *Guide des privatisables*, Albin Michel, Paris.

Dean, J. (1951), *Managerial Economics*, Prentice-Hall International, Hemel Hempstead.

Delors, J. and Clisthène (1988), *La France par l'Europe*, Grasset, Paris.

Drucker, P. (1969), *The Age of Discontinuity: guidelines to our changing society*, Heinemann, London.

Fraser, R. (1988), *Privatization: the UK Experience*, Longman, Harlow.

Frommer, J. and McCormick, J. (1990), *Transformations in French Business*, Quorum, New York.

Garrison, T. (1991), *European Business Policy*, ELM Publications, Huntingdon.

Godt, P. (1989), *Policy-Making in France*, Pinter, London.

Haigh, N. (1987), *EEC Environmental Policy and Britain*, 2nd ed., Longman, Harlow.

Hall, P. (1986), *Governing the Economy: the politics of state intervention in Britain and France*, Cambridge: Polity Press.

Handy, C. (1976), *Understanding Organisations*, Penguin Books, Harmondsworth.

Herzog, P. and Dimicoli, Y. (1989), *Europe 92: construire autrement et autre chose*, Messidor/Editions Sociales, Paris.

Hofstede, G. (1980), *Culture's Consequences*, Sage, London.

Johnson, G. and Scholes, K. (1988), *Exploring Corporate Strategy*, Prentice Hall, London.

Kennedy, P. (1989), *The Rise and Fall of the Great Powers*, Fontana Press, London.

Kerin, R. A. and Peterson, R. A. (1983), *Perspectives in Strategic Marketing Management*, Allyn and Bacon, Boston.

Landes, D. S. (1969), *The Unbound Prometheus: technological change in Western Europe from 1750 to the present*, Cambridge University Press, Cambridge.

Lane, C. (1989), *Management and Labour in Europe*, Edward Elgar, Aldershot.

Lodge, J. (1989), *The European Community and the Challenge of the Future*, Pinter, London.

MacGregor, I. with Tyler, R. (1987), *The Enemies Within: the story of the Miners' Strike, 1984–5*, Fontana/Collins, Glasgow.

Machin, H. and Wright, V., eds (1985), *Economic Policy and Policy-Making under the Mitterrand Presidency 1981–1984*, Pinter, London.

Maclean, M. and Howorth, J., eds (1991), *Europeans on Europe: transnational visions of a new continent*, Macmillan, London.

Magniadas, J. (1991), *Le Patronat*, Messidor/Editions sociales, Paris.

Maisonrouge, J. (1988), *Inside IBM: a European's story*, Fontana/Collins, London.

Malandain, G. and Tavernier, Y. (1991), *Pour sauver l'eau*, Rino, Paris.

Markowitz, H. M. (1959), *Portfolio Selection: efficient diversification of investment*, John Wiley and Jones, New York.

Miles, R. E. and Snow, C. C. (1978), *Organizational Strategy, Structure and Process*, McGraw-Hill, New York.

Minc, A. (1989), *La Grande Illusion*, Grasset, Paris.

Morin, E. (1987), *Penser l'Europe*, UGE, Paris.

Naudet, J.-Y. (1989), *L'Economie française face aux défis*, Economica, Paris.

Observatoire des Stratégies industrielles (1990), *Marché unique, marché multiple*, Economica, Paris.

Ohmae, K. (1990), *The Borderless World: power and strategy in the interlinked economy*, Collins, London.

Ohmae, K. (1987), *The Mind of the Strategist*, Penguin Books, Harmondsworth.

Otley, D. (1987), *Accounting Control and Organizational Behaviour*, Heinemann, London.

Pappas, J. L., Brigham, E. F., and Shipley, B. (1983), *Managerial Economics*, Cassell Education Ltd, London.

Peters, T. J. and Waterman, R. H. (1982), *In Search of Excellence*, Harper and Row, New York.

Ramanadham, V. V. (1988), *Privatisation in the UK*, Routledge, London.

Randlesome, C. et al. (1990), *Business Cultures in Europe*, Heinemann, London.

Rose, C. (1990), *The Dirty Man of Europe: the great British pollution scandal*, Simon and Schuster, London.

Schein, E. (1985), *Organisational Culture and Leadership*, Jossey Bass, London.

Scherer, F. M. (1980), *Industrial Market Structure and Economic Performance*, 2nd ed., Rand McNally, London.

Servan-Schreiber, J.-L. (1990), *Le Métier de patron*, Fayard, Paris.

Sharp, M. and Holmes, P. (1990), *Strategies for New Technology: case studies from Britain and France*, Phillip Allan, New York.

Sharp, M. and Shearman, C. (1987), *European Technological Collaboration*, Routledge and Kegan Paul, London.

Siedentopf, H. and Ziller, J., eds. (1988), *Making European Policies Work: the implementation of Community legislation in Member States*, Sage, London.

Simon, H. A. (1960), *The New Science of Management Decision*, Harper and Row, New York.

Stout, R. (1980), *Management or Control?: the organizational challenge*, Indiana University Press, Bloomington.

Articles and papers

Berger, S. (1987), 'French business from transition to transition', in Ross, G., Hoffmann, S. and Malzacher, S., eds, *The Mitterrand Experiment*, Oxford University Press, Oxford and New York.

Berger, S. (1981), 'Lame ducks and national champions: industrial policy in the Fifth Republic', in Andrews, W. G. and Hoffmann, S., eds, *The Fifth Republic at Twenty*, State University of New York Press, New York.

Berger, S. (1987). 'Liberalism reborn: the new liberal synthesis in France', in Howorth, J. and Ross, G., eds., *Contemporary France: a review of interdisciplinary studies*, vol. 1, Pinter, London, pp. 84–108.

Bournois, F. and Chauchat, J.-H. (1990), 'Managing Managers in Europe', *European Management Journal*, vol. 8, no. 1, pp. 3–18.

Bowers, J. and O'Donnell, K. (1987), 'Privatisation and the control of pollution', University of Leeds School of Economic Studies Discussion Paper Series, no. 87/10.

Bowers, J., O' Donnell, K. and Ogden, S. (1988), 'Privatisation of the water supply: some outstanding issues', *University of Leeds School of Economics Discussion Paper Series*.

Bowers, J., O'Donnell, K. and Whatmore, S. (1988), *Liquid Assets: the likely effects of privatisation of the water authorities on wildlife habitats and landscape*, CPRE, RSPB, WWF.

Butt Philip, A. A. S. (1988), 'Implementing the European Internal Market: problems and prospects', *Royal Institute for International Affairs Discussion Papers Series*, no. 5.

Butt Philip, A. A. S. (1991), 'Westminster versus Brussels — the last crusade?', in Maclean, M. and Howorth, J., *Europeans on Europe: transnational visions of a new continent*, op. cit.

Cerny, P. G. (1989), 'From *dirigisme* to deregulation? the case of financial markets', in Godt, P., ed., op. cit.

Charbonnel, L. (1988), 'Les aspects juridiques de la protection et de la gestion des milieux aquatiques', *La Gestion de l'eau*, Annales des Mines, pp. 93–5.

Glynn, D. (1988), 'Economic regulation of the privatized water industry', in Johnson, C., ed., *Lloyds Bank Annual Review: privatization and ownership*, Pinter, London.

Harper, W. R. (1988), 'Privatisation in the water sector', in Ramanadham, V. V., op. cit.

Hayward, J. (1976), 'Institutional inertia and political impetus in France and Britain', *European Journal of Political Research*, 4.

Hofstede, G. (1985), 'The cultural perspective', in Brakel, A., ed., *People and Organisations Interacting*, John Wiley, New York.

Holcblat, N. and Tavernier, J.-L. (1989), 'Entre 1979 et 1986, la France a perdu des parts de marché industriel', *Economie et Statistique*, 217–8, pp. 37–49.

Hoffmann, S. (1987), 'France and Europe: the dichotomy of autonomy and cooperation', in Howorth, J. and Ross, G., eds., *Contemporary France: a journal of interdisciplinary studies*, vol. 1, op. cit., pp. 46–54.

Leynaud, G. (1988), 'Les bases scientifiques de la protection et de la gestion des milieux aquatiques et de leurs peuplements', *La Gestion de l'eau*, Annales des Mines, pp. 96–105.

Maclean, M. (1987), 'The future of privatisation in France: a crisis of confidence?', *Modern and Contemporary France*, no. 31, pp. 1–9.

Maclean, M. (1989), 'Privatisation and people's capitalism in France: old habits in new guises?', *Contemporary French Civilization*, vol. XIII, no. 1, pp. 1–18.

Maclean, M. (1991), 'The Unfinished Chrysalis: market forces and protectionist reflexes in France', in Maclean, M. and Howorth, J., *Europeans on Europe: transnational visions of a new continent*, op. cit., pp. 21–39.

Ohmae, K. (1990), 'Global logic of strategic alliances', *EuroBusiness*, vol. 2, no. 2, pp. 19–23.

Porter, M. E. (1979), 'How competitive forces shape strategy', *Harvard Business Review*.

Rees, J. and Synnott, M. (1986). 'Are the Water Authorities an attractive prospect?', *Public Money*, pp. 46–51.

Smith, W. R. (1989), '"We can make the Ariane, but we can't make washing machines": the State and industrial performance in post-war France', in Howorth, J. and Ross, G., eds, *Contemporary France: a review of interdisciplinary studies*, vol. 3, Pinter, London.

Stoffaës, C. (1989), 'Industrial policy and the State', in Godt, P., op. cit.

Tenaillon, P. L. (1988), 'Les évolutions de la gestion de l'eau', *La Gestion de l'eau*, Annales des Mines, pp. 143–5.

Verba, S. (1965), 'Comparative political culture', in Pye, L. and Verba, S, eds., *Political Culture and Political Development*, Princeton University Press, Princeton.

Woolcock, S. (1989), 'European Mergers: national or community controls?', *Royal Institute for International Affairs Discussion Papers Series*, no. 15.

Woodward, N. (1988), '"Managing" cultural change on privatisation', in Ramandham, V. V., op. cit.

Numerous articles from the *Daily Telegraph*, *The Economist*, the *Financial Times*, the *Guardian*, the *Independent*, the *Independent on Sunday*, the *Observer*, *The Times*, *L'Expansion*, *Libération* and *Le Monde* are referred to in the main body of the text.

Index